Promoting Student Learning and Student Development at a Distance

Student Affairs Concepts and Practices for Televised Instruction and Other Forms of Distance Learning

Alan M. Schwitzer
OLD DOMINION UNIVERSITY

Julie R. Ancis
GEORGIA STATE UNIVERSITY

Nina Brown
OLD DOMINION UNIVERSITY

American College Personnel Association

Copyright © 2001 by the
American College Personnel Association.

Distributed by University Press of America,® Inc.
4720 Boston Way, Lanham, Maryland 20706

Library of Congress Cataloging-in-Publication Data

Schwitzer, Alan M.
Promoting student learning and student development at a
distance : student affairs concepts and practices for televised
instruction and other forms of distance learning /
Alan M. Schwitzer, Julie R. Ancis, Nina Brown.
p.   cm
Includes bibliographical references.
l. Distance education—United States. 2. Educational technology—
United States. I. Ancis, Julie R. II. Brown, Nina W. III. Title.
LC5805 .S37   2000   378.1'75'0973—dc21   00-049585 CIP

ISBN 1-883485-21-5 (cloth : alk. paper)
ISBN 1-883485-22-3 (pbk. : alk. paper)

⊖™ The paper used in this publication meets the minimum
requirements of American National Standard for Information
Sciences—Permanence of Paper for Printed Library Materials,
ANSI Z39.48—1984

ACPA Media Board

100966

Contents

Chapter 5
Student Learning: Student Affairs Professionals as
Distance Educators

vi

Preface

This book answers four questions about promoting student learning and development at a distance:

1. What is distance learning as it is defined and practiced in the United States?
2. Who are distance learners and what are their needs?
3. What student learning and student development approaches and practices are necessary for effective distance student services and supportive distance communities?
4. What student learning and student development approaches and practices are necessary for effective electronic classrooms and academic programs?

Plan of the Book

Part I: Higher Education and Distance Learning in the United States

Part I introduces distance learning concepts and terminology, describes the major trends influencing American distance learning, and provides an overview of the current distance learning theoretical and practitioner knowledge-base. Part I begins a discussion of the ways in which distance learning systems for delivering higher education continue to influence the work of professionals who are responsible for college student learning and development.

Chapter 1. Higher Education and Distance Learning in the United States: An Introduction

Chapter 1 provides an overview and definition of distance learning. Current trends in higher education which influence American distance learning are introduced, including: calls for more efficient delivery of higher education; greater focus on educational missions and meeting broader constituent needs; emergence of information technology delivery systems; and successful distance learning programs in Britain and Canada. Distance learning formats are introduced, including: online teaching and electronic college courses; broadcast television classes and telelcourses; and interactive audio-video classrooms. The importance of distance learning for student development professionals is highlighted.

Chapter 2. Higher Education and Distance Learning in the United States: Knowledge Base and Practice

Chapter 2 introduces distance learning as it is practiced in the United States. The American "pragmatic eclectic" approach is described, and compared with the British Open University model. Major themes in the American distance learning literature are reviewed, including: defining the field, the role of learner variables, the changing role of faculty, and interactivity. Critical roles for student development are emphasized.

Part II: Student Development and Learning at a Distance

Part II builds on the foundation of the knowledge-base introduced in Chapters 1 and 2 with a thorough discussion of the issues important to student affairs practice in distance settings. First, factors and practices influencing distance student adjustment, learning, and development are reviewed, and student affairs responses to distance student needs are explored. Next, factors and practices influencing student learning inside "electronic classrooms"—and new roles for student affairs professionals as distance educators are explored. Learning-centered instructional principles, academic program design, and assessment are discussed.

Chapter 3. Distance Learners: Characteristics and Needs

Chapter 3 describes the characteristics and learner variables that tend to define the distance classroom population. These include: age, maturity, and development; cognitive developmental factors; gender, ethnicity, and geography; motivation, goals, and lifestyle choices; and academic familiarity, prior learning experiences, and anxiety. Teaching principles are introduced that are responsive to learner needs, such as: enhancing the meaningfulness of course content, creating a conducive interpersonal class climate, and attending to the cultural context of teaching methods. Student services responses are presented that promote adjustment and retention, such as: admissions, registrar, and orientation services; advising, career counseling, and program planning; psychological counseling; and instrumental support.

Chapter 4. Student Development:
Creating Community at a Distance

Chapter 4 first briefly reviews the influence of community support on college student adjustment, learning, and development. This chapter reviews the roles of teacher support and peer affiliation on learning outcomes; learner help-seeking and the role of student services in learner success; and the specific role of social climate and support services in the adjustment, retention, and success of non-traditional, first-generation, ethnic minority, and at-risk students. This chapter also summarizes current research applying student development principles to distance learners. Components of a strategy for creating student affairs and building community at a distance are then presented. These are: including the distance learner in the life of the university, consumer services, faculty support of distance learners, peer affiliation at a distance, group-oriented services, and involving institutional leaders. This chapter emphasizes student support practices at a distance.

Chapter 5. Student Learning: Achieving Outcomes at a Distance

Chapter 5 introduces new roles for student development professionals as distance educators who are likely to be more involved in the academic life of the institution than they are typically are on the main campus. Teaching methods that emphasize active learning will be explored, along with the need to combine audio and video teaching methods. The new or expanded roles include: faculty development provider, academic liaison, program designer, and outcome evaluator. Chapter 5 then presents a case example drawn from one institution's experience illustrates the design of distance student services.

Afterward

The Afterward provides a brief conclusion.

A Handful of Complementary Resources

The following books and journals complement our own book by discussing traditional student affairs work, addressing academic programming, presenting consumer choices, and forming a new professional literature in a time-period of rapid advancement of technology-enhanced higher education. Together with this book, these selections will provide professionals with a solid introduction to changing methods of delivering the college and university experience. Our choice for a small personal library of distance education resources includes the following:

American Center for the Study of Distance Education. (1987-present). *The American Journal of Distance Education.* University Park, PA: Authors, College of Education, Pennsylvania State University. This national, peer-reviewed periodical was established in 1987 and is published three times per year. The main focus of this professional journal is on the use of electronic instruction methods, telecommunications and multimedia systems in the delivery of education in universities and colleges, business and industry, the military, as well as elementary and secondary schools. It publishes research and practice articles, and includes discussion and debate about the distance learning enterprise. While the journal's focus is on distance learning across educational settings, there is significant emphasis on colleges and universities.

Baier, J. L., and Strong, T. S. (1994). *Technology in student affairs: Issues, applications, and trends.* Lanham, MD: American College Personnel Association. This book provides a comprehensive guide to technology in student affairs on traditional campuses. Since many student affairs divisions have introduced advanced information and computer systems, this book is designed primarily to assist student affairs practitioners, graduate students, and faculty in applying new information technologies and telecommunication technologies to programs on an institution's main campus. Topics include computer software, CD-Rom technology, database applications for academic advising, technology-driven resources for teaching-learning programs, and methods for technology-enhanced counseling, career planning, and student life programs. While this text does not discuss distance learning *per se*, nearly all of the topics covered will be valuable for student affairs work with distance learners.

Cyrs, T. E. (Ed.). (1997). *Teaching and learning at a distance: What it takes to effectively design, deliver, and evaluate programs*. San Francisco: Jossey-Bass. This book provides an introduction to academic course design and college teaching in the distance learning environment. Since successful teaching and learning at a distance requires more than advanced technology, this book is designed primarily to assist college and university faculty who are making the transition from traditional classroom teaching to distance education. Topics include developing competence and new skills for teaching via television, telephone, and Internet. The book also addresses important distance faculty concerns such as teaching evaluations, copyright, and digital library resources. One chapter discusses learner development. This text complements our focus on student development with an emphasis on the instructional design principles that are needed to make distance teaching work.

Levine, T. K. (1992). *Going the distance: A handbook for developing distance degree programs*. This guidebook was produced by the PBS Adult Learning Service in cooperation with a special project, the Annenberg/CPB Project. As a handbook, it provides a comprehensive framework for design, implementation, and evaluation of one pilot academic program. As such, it provides one interesting case example that might be illuminating for administrators and faculty in the "start up" phase of an institution's distance learning efforts. This book provides brief, practical discussions of trends in distance learning degree programs; marketing, accreditation, and admissions issues associated with establishing a new distance learning degree program; selection and reward of distance faculty; implementation of support services for distance learners; and cost-effectiveness of distance education programs.

Peterson's. (1998). *The electronic university: A guide to distance learning programs (2nd Ed.)*. This consumer catalog is a comprehensive source-book of distance learning and distance education programs of accredited colleges and universities in the United States. It includes descriptions of higher education programs that are delivered to "off-site" students through the use of technologies such as cable and satellite tele vision, video and audiotapes, computer conferencing, and other means of electronic delivery. The catalog includes credit and non-credit courses, academic degree, and professional certification programs. Each profile— of more than 100 institutions—includes consumer information about programs of study, special programs, faculty, admissions, tuition and fees, financial aid, and application procedures. Contacts at each institution also are given, including mail and email addresses, telephone and fax numbers, and web sites.

Part I

Higher Education and Distance Learning in the United States

Part I introduces the delivery of higher education in the United States via distance learning. American distance education takes a pragmatic approach that has been influenced by distance learning successes internationally and the availability of new technologies, as well as social, political, and economic trends. There is a growing distance learning literature that so far has focused mainly on establishing the discipline, but is moving increasingly toward theoretical and empirical studies of distance learning practices and outcomes. The focus of Part I is on what college student affairs professionals and teaching faculty need to know about American distance education. Chapter 1 provides a technical introduction to the world of distance education. Chapter 2 follows with a review of the major themes from the current distance learning literature.

Chapter 1

Higher Education and Distance Learning in the United States: An Introduction

Using new telecommunications capabilities and advanced information technologies, American learners today are enrolling in college courses and completing entire academic degree programs without ever setting foot on their institution's main campus. Increasingly, learners connected by computer interaction and the Internet, satellite, and telephone and electronic facsimile machines are participating in electronic classrooms and information-age college experiences at distant campus sites, at their businesses and workplaces, on military bases and naval ships, and in their homes. Certainly, high school seniors who go on to pursue "four critical years" of traditional learning and developmental experiences on conventional college campuses will continue to be a major segment of the higher education market in the United States; however, there is already widespread evidence of what the National Education Association (NEA) called an "exploding" (Oldenburg, 1996, p. B5) distance learning trend.

Peterson's Guides now publishes *The electronic university: A guide to distance learning programs*, listing approximately 100 degree programs and certificate courses offered through some form of distance learning. In a two-week span in 1996, the *Washington Post* carried articles about televised university education, computerized college courses, and utilization of the Internet in "plugged-in" classrooms. *The American Journal of Distance Education* began publication in 1987 as a professional outlet for research, theory, and practice articles that form a foundation for an emerging distance learning discipline. The American Psychological Association's Division on the Teaching of Psychology sponsored a symposium (Ancis, 1996) on distance learning at the 1996 APA convention in Toronto, Canada, and then in 1998 sponsored an entire conference dedicated to teaching and technology. The American College Student Personnel Association sponsors an increasing number of programs on topics related to distance education and student development at its annual conventions—and includes a regular "Electronic Campus" feature in its professional magazine, *About Campus* (American College Personnel Association, 1996-present).

It appears that reality is beginning to live up to earlier hype about technology-enhanced learning. This book introduces distance learning concepts and discusses implications of distance learning trends for professionals who are (or will be) responsible for student learning and student development at a distance.

Trends and Influences on Distance Learning in the United States

Several factors have contributed to the emergence of electronic college courses and online instruction, broadcast television and teleclasses, interactive electronic classrooms, and the use of new technologies on-campus, as alternative methods of delivering American higher education. First, longer-standing distance education programs internationally have proven successful. In particular, the British Open University is commonly cited as American distance learning's predecessor (Zigarell, 1991). Second, institutions in the United States have experienced increased pressure to deliver higher education more efficiently, and to pay more attention to the needs of constituents (Blyn & Zoerner, 1982; Guskin, 1997). Distance education is one alternative response to these pressures. Finally, the recent availability of advanced communications and information technology provided the necessary mechanisms for American ventures into new ways of delivering higher education (Duning, Van Kekerix, & Zabobowski, 1993).

Distance Learning Around the World

Distance learning established a foothold internationally in the early 1970s with the success of the Open University in the United Kingdom. Originating in Great Britain, the Open University concept was first proposed in 1963, greatly debated for nearly a decade, implemented in 1970, and up-and- running by 1971 (Ferguson, 1976). The Open University used British Broadcasting Company (BBC) radio and television broadcasts, along with pre-packaged print and other academic materials, to deliver university-level instruction to learners' homes.

The Open University broke away from traditional British higher education in several ways (Ferguson, 1976; Perry, 1977; Tunstall, 1973). The British Open University was designed to meet the social/political goal of democratizing university access. Open University instruction reached a wider learner constituency than traditional campus-based institutions in the U. K. While other British institutions relied on a system of entrance qualifications, distance learners could enter the Open University without formally qualifying. Further, unlike traditional college students in Britain, Open University students tended to be non-traditionally aged adult learners in their late twenties, thirties, and forties who were completing college degrees part-time while maintaining their full-time employment. The Open University did not follow a traditional academic timetable. These learners pursued an education at their own pace, usually completing a degree program in two to eight years.

Technologically, the Open University relied on broadcast courses and some teleclasses (delivered through the BBC), specially developed course-specific books, and other self-paced learning materials (early "home experimental kits" even included on-loan microscopes for some science courses!) to be completed and returned in person or by mail. Computer applications enhanced the system. Local "study centers" were established in geographically accessible sites to provide part-time tutoring and student counseling services (advising, career planning, counseling support).

In addition to reaching a wider student population, the Open University was designed to be an economical method of delivering higher education. The Open University introduced new, more efficient teaching arrangements and student support services—and reduced the need for on-campus residences, academic buildings and campus construction, and student services. Earliest estimates were that the Open University cost "less than a third" of equivalent traditional British institutions (Wagner, 1973). The Open University demonstrated a method for reaching more learners, and doing so more cost-effectively, than traditional universities.

The Open University concept has been adopted extensively around the world. Australia used public-private partnerships to establish a widespread distance education system and distance learning is used to bring higher education to adult learners in Canada (Reddy, 1988; Smith & Kelly, 1987). European distance learning examples based on the Open University model are found in Germany and Spain (Reddy, 1988). Asian and Pacific Rim examples include national distance learning programs in China, India, Indonesia, Japan, Korea, Pakistan, and Thailand (Evans & Nation, 1989; Reddy, 1988).

Cost-Effectiveness: Public Scrutiny and Calls for Efficiency

Because distance education appeared to be successful in Britain, Australia, Canada, and elsewhere, an interest in applying distance learning methods to the delivery of higher education in the United States followed in the mid-1980s and gained momentum in the 1990s. Independent study programs and isolated distance education efforts existed previously in the United States; however, the distance learning enterprise did not yet have a significant impact on American community colleges, colleges, and universities. For example, it was in 1982 that Empire State College of State University of New York, an institutional pioneer, first offered distance education courses. By 1996, 1,400 students were enrolled in almost 200 distance learning courses at Empire (Peterson's Guides, 1998). The printing of the first volume of the *American Journal of Distance Education* (a national, refereed journal managed by the Office of Distance Education of the College of Education at The Pennsylvania State University) in 1987-1988 seems to be a reasonable place to mark the formal beginning of an American distance learning discipline.

One reason for the growing interest in distance learning was the increasing public scrutiny, declining public support, and the corresponding pressure experienced by American institutions to deliver higher education more efficiently and economically. Higher education in the United States has experienced declines in budgets, state funding, and other resources (Blyn & Zoerner, 1982; Guskin, 1997). One institutional response to persistent budget restrictions has been resource reallocation in the form of cutbacks in selected areas, which often result in personnel and program reductions or eliminations.

A second institutional response to the demand for greater accountability in exchange for funding has been heightened emphasis on long-range planning that ties resources to the efficient production of positive student learning outcomes (Schwitzer, 1997b). According to this "management perspective" (Kozloff, 1987, p. 419), resources are allocated on the basis of measurable ratios between money put into an institution or specific program, and resultant academic outcomes. Funding decisions are made on the basis of an institution's "efficiency" and effectiveness. Outcomes are operationalized as student grades, retention rates, academic credits earned toward graduation across cumulative semesters of enrollment, graduation rates after 4 and 5 years of enrollment, and post-graduation placement rates in work settings or graduate and professional schools.

The management perspective of accountability coexists in American higher education with student-centered perspectives that put more emphasis on student development variables and successful program implementation (Kozloff, 1987, Schwitzer, 1997b). These perspectives contrast and complement the management perspective by focusing on the overall college experience, and achieving adjustment outcomes, developmental change, and students' learning goals. As a result, there is sometimes resistance to management systems of accountability —because administrative decisions and methods of evaluation driven solely by resource criteria may not allow sufficient room to address important student development variables or key programs and services of the overall college experience—and debate about whether management perspectives adequately address quality of learning and developmental experiences (Astin, 1985; Kozloff, 1987).

However, increasingly, accreditation bodies and state legislatures require institutions and specific departments to demonstrate intended student outcomes as part of their planning and funding process (Ewell & Boyer, 1988). For academic departments, the management perspective means demonstrating the strongest resource-to-student outcome ratio possible (e.g., larger enrollments and better graduation rates, with fewer faculty and dollars). The management perspective also requires student services to demonstrate cost-effectiveness. For example, college counseling centers have experienced pressures to increase efficiency or limit services in the face of increasing demand (Bishop, 1990), and to demonstrate cost-effectiveness of counseling services by evaluating their impact on institutional retention rates and academic success (Giddan & Weiss, 1990).

As the British Open University demonstrated, distance education formats have the potential to reach more students with fewer faculty, only limited face-to-face services, and fewer on-campus resources such as classrooms and residence halls (realizing, of course, that start-up costs are required for purchasing technology, training staff and faculty, licensing and initially purchasing broadcast time or Internet access). Illustrating the institutional benefits of distance education in terms of revenue and public perceptions, a newspaper editorial reviewing advances in Old Dominion University's distance learning program said the following:

> . . . The day will come, we'd guess, when the number of long-distance ODU students exceeds the number of students on ODU's Norfolk campus. That would be good news for Virginia taxpayers if only because the distance students' tuitions and fees more than cover the cost to provide the courses. "It's a source of revenue that is just as real as a foundation giving us a grant," says ODU President James V. Koch. (Sorensen, A. July 30, 1998).

In this context, distance learning provides a method for "industrializing" higher education (Keegan, 1986). Described from the perspective of an economist, distance education is an industrialization process that uses a division of labor and technology to mass produce high-quality teaching and learning (Keegan, 1986; Peters, 1971). In turn, the climate of public scrutiny and cost-effectiveness experienced by American higher education provided momentum for the distance learning enterprise in the United States, since it had the potential to be one efficient alternative for delivering higher education and producing student outcomes.

Meeting Constituent Needs: Public Scrutiny and Calls for Responsiveness

A second component of the recent public scrutiny and accountability trends in higher education has been consistent pressure on colleges and universities to emphasize student learning needs and educational attainment as primary goals. Institutions have experienced public pressure not just to operate more cost-effectively, but also to operate in new ways that more clearly emphasize undergraduate experiences and the educational needs of a wider range of constituent learners (Bennett, 1984; Wingspread Group on Higher Education, 1993). Attention in American higher education has refocused on increased learner access, student productivity, and educational attainment.

Responses from academic departments have included reallocating resources based on consumer demand, offering some classes at off-campus academic centers, expanding continuing education, and offering more coursework through weekend colleges and other nontraditional scheduling. There also has been an increase in conducting outcome assessment of academic programs to measure the quality of student experiences and learning outcomes (Osborne & House, 1995).

Student affairs divisions have responded with new frameworks for practice that clearly emphasize student learning. Contemporary frameworks for student services work assume that "if learning is the primary measure of institutional productivity . . . what and how much students learn also must be the criteria by which the value of student affairs is judged" (American College Personnel Association, 1994, p. 2). The focus of such outcome assessment is to show the extent to which student services result in *learning*—increases in knowledge, understanding, or intellectual complexity, and in *development*—applying learning gains to life situations (Bloland, Stamatakos, & Roger, 1996; Schwitzer, 1998).

Once again demonstrated by the British Open University, "industrializing" higher education through distance learning has the potential to respond to constituent learning needs and educational attainment goals by reaching more learners at one time, using a wider range of delivery modes, and more flexibly fitting higher education into the life situations of an institution's consumers. The newspaper editorial reviewing the "Teletechnet" distance learning program at Old Dominion University illustrated the institutional benefits of distance education in terms of gaining public support by better meeting constituent needs:

[Cost-effectiveness] is not the only benefit. ODU [serves regional] residents who couldn't go away to college because of jobs or other ties. Teletechnet serves the same function, but over a far larger area.

For example, Clarence Simington, Jr., a Martinsville police officer, lived [a prohibitive] 90 minutes from Virginia Tech . . . Through

Teletechet, he earned an ODU bachelor's degree . . . having to drive but 10 minutes to [an electronic] classroom . . .

Teletechnet is a bargain for students, because they don't have to move to attend college and they pay slightly less than on-campus students . . .

To reach workers and others who cannot attend classes during the week, the school offers what it calls a Weekend College. Students [who don't choose distance learning] are commuting to the Weekend College from as far away as Alexandria and Fredericksburg. Teletechnet adds to ODU's admirable reputation as an institution that finds new ways to serve . . . (Sorensen, July 30, 1998).

In this context, distance learning provides one potential tool for colleges and universities seeking to address the needs of changing consumer constituencies. Distance learning potentially provides alternative methods of delivering higher education to traditional and non-traditional undergraduate and graduate students, continuing education for learners across the life-span, and employee and worker training in business and industry (Moore, 1988). To realize these potentials, institutions must use new technologies not just to achieve "bottom line" goals associated with the management perspective, but also to ensure quality distance learning experiences. As institutions find new ways to serve, they must create distance learning programs that ensure that their new constituents: (a) receive educational programs of equal quality to main campus offering, (b) have easy access to learning resources that meet their needs, and (c) are supported by well-planned university experiences and services (Beaudoin, 1990; Garrison & Shale, 1987).

Availability of New Technologies

The success of established distance learning programs internationally and the pressure for more efficient, responsive higher education together set the stage for American distance learning. However, the final essential element was the emergence in the 1980s and 1990s of new, advanced, increasingly affordable telecommunications and information technologies that could provide the hardware for "industrializing" or "mass producing" higher education.

The components of advanced technologies are best understood as falling into three categories (Duning, Van Kekerix, & Zaborowski, 1993):

hardware, software, and transport. *Hardware* refers to the equipment, or "machinery" that is utilized in telecommunications or computer operations. The hardware of distance learning is comprised of personal computers, audio-video monitors, wiring, cameras, and microphones, as well as telephones and facsimile machines. Computer *software* refers to systems for directing, operating, controlling, and manipulating hardware. *Transport* refers to electronic methods for sending and receiving programming between educators and learners at disparate locations.

Different modes of delivering distance education rely on different hardware developments, software advances, and improvements in transport. Some distance learning modes capitalize on the capabilities of new technologies for *networking people*—for electronically linking people so they can communicate and interact. When the purpose is networking people, the hardware most often is a personal computer. Both interactive communications and instructional software are used. For example, online courses and some electronic classes rely on new networking capabilities for faculty-learner and learner-learner interaction. The instructor and students may require different technological capabilities for communicating. For instance, the instructor may need the ability to create a Website or establish a chat room, whereas students need only the ability to access or enter the learning formats provided (Ancis, 1996; Anderson, Benjamin, Busiel, & Paredes-Holt, 1998).

Other distance learning modes capitalize on the capabilities of new technologies for *combining locations*, or for bringing people at geographically separate sites together in a "real time" audio-visual classroom. When the purpose is combining locations, hardware and transport include electronic telecommunications systems, cameras and microphones, and linking mechanisms such as fiber optics and microwaves. For example, broadcast courses and interactive audio-video classrooms rely on new methods of combining locations to deliver instruction and create an interactive "facsimile" of the college classroom experience. Different technologies may be required at the *origination site* versus *reception sites*. For instance, when one-way video is used, monitors but not cameras are needed at reception sites. Similarly, when sites are separated by great distances, transport needs are different than when all the sites are located somewhere on-campus.

Finally, electronic technologies are capable of being *integrated*, producing combinations that can meet the needs of different learning environments. For example, interactive classrooms may utilize one way video and two-way audio, or two-way audio and video. Classes broadcast on commercial television might include online instruction components to enhance the one-way delivery of instructional material through greater interaction among learners. Even in the simplest cases, prepackaged electronic courses often require communication with the instructor via email, telephone, and fax. In turn, the emergence of new technologies—and the capacity for integrating them to meet individualized needs—allowed American institutions the ability and flexibility to network people and combine locations in such a way that has made distance education goals achievable.

Defining Distance Learning

Distance learning is the provision of academic courses and entire degree programs when instructor and students are geographically separated. We use the term, *distance learning*, throughout this book because the emphasis is on a *learner*-centered system with most educational, teaching, and supportive activity focused on *facilitating learning* among students at a distance (Beaudoin, 1990). An equally common term is "distance education."

Distance learning in the United States is not entirely new. As early as 1939, the Detroit public schools were experimenting with teaching in urban settings by radio (Schwitzer, 1997a). Institutions such as the University of Michigan and American University began using televised instruction in the late 1940s and early 1950s (Zigarell, 1991). Correspondence courses have been available through American colleges and universities for more than 100 years (Peterson's Guides, 1998). However, in today's world, a wide range of technologies are used to bridge geographic distances by electronically delivering educational programs to off-site learners. Distance learning can be used to augment traditional campus classroom learning (for example, professors may establish Web sites or chat rooms that allow for student discussions via computer networking), provide continuing education and professional certification courses (for example, offering teleconferences in workplaces), or deliver for-credit college courses and degree programs (for example, offering an Introduction to Sociology course or entire General Education program via commercial cable television).

Technology-driven distance learning as it is practiced today is somewhat different from other distance learning approaches where the student is geographically separated from the institution, such as traditional forms of "independent study" or learning by "correspondence". Traditional correspondence courses, without the enhancements of information- and communications-technologies, usually rely exclusively on the students' ability to learn by themselves—and therefore do not require class attendance or provide opportunities for real interactions with a professor or other learners (Tunstall, 1973; Perry, 1977; Beaudoin, 1990). On the other hand, when distance-learning approaches center around information- and communication-technologies, they provide a variety of faculty-learner, learner-learner, and learner-institution interactions—and may require periodic campus visits or regular "class" attendance at distance sites, in specially wired classrooms, at work or at home. Technology-driven distance learning methods almost always include critical opportunities for learner-instructor and learner-learner interactions that attempt to create a *facsimile* of the college course experience which is more accessible and more convenient for an institution's consumer-constituency.

Modes of distance education delivery differ along four characteristics. These are: 1) the type of technology required; 2) the degree of faculty-learner interactivity, 3) the degree of learner-learner interactivity, and 4) access to student support services and resources. Each characteristic has implications for the distance learner's satisfaction and academic success (see Table 1.1 for a summary).

Type of Technology Required

Colleges and universities use a variety of technologies to deliver distance education. Correspondingly, distance learners must have access to required technology in order to enroll in distance programs. For example, students would need a television and VCR when enrolled in telecourses offered through commercial broadcast or cable television, and they must have access to a computer and Internet connection for Web-based courses. Some distance learning technologies require students to attend class in specially-wired remote classrooms, usually located close-by their homes or workplaces. Nearly all forms of distance learning require that students have access to a combination of telephone, fax, email, and perhaps overnight mail service, in order to communicate with the instructor and interact with other learners.

Table 1.1
Modes of Distance Learning Delivery and their Characteristics

Mode of Delivery	Brief Description	Technology Required	Characteristics			
			Faculty-Learner Interactivity	Learner-Learner Interactivity	Student Services
Technology-Assisted Learning On Campus	Faculty and students interact electronically outside of class	Faculty/student access to email, Web, fax, or telephone	Heightened	Heightened	Full Range
Electronic Courses	Pre-packaged self-paced courses formatted for computer software	Personal computer	Low Asynchronous	None	Academic Support/ Career
Online Instruction	Electronic courses home-delivered via Web/Internet	Personal computer, Internet	Moderate Synchronous/ Asynchronous	Moderate Synchronous/ Asynchronous	Academic Support/ Career
Broadcast Television	Class lectures home-delivered via broadcast or cable television	Origination site on-campus, television and VCR at home	Low Asynchronous	None	Academic Support/ Career
Telecourses	Class lectures delivered to receptor classes	Origination and receptor sites, One-way technology	Low Asynchronous	High In-person	Academic Support/ Career
Interactive Audio-Video Classrooms	Multiple-site class meeting via two-way audio/video	Origination and receptor sites, Two-way technology	High Synchronous	High Synchronous	Wider Range of Services

Technological requirements extend beyond *access* to equipment. Distance students' comfort level and skills also influence learning. When distance students are uncomfortable about utilizing computer-based instructional technologies (Overbaugh, 1994), or apprehensive about communicating via telecommunications technology (Wolcott, 1995), they can experience feelings of anxiety and alienation that interfere with their ability to learn. As a result, distance students first must develop reasonable competencies and comfort levels with the necessary technology before they can effectively engage in learning.

Faculty-Learner Interactivity

Teaching faculty have been referred to as the sometimes "neglected resource" in technology-based distance learning, since technological advances and the hard-wiring of electronic courses are often the main foci in designing these types of distance programs (Dillon & Walsh, 1992, p. 5). While technology initially sets the stage for delivering electronic distance learning, faculty-learner interaction remains a critical factor in student satisfaction and success (Fulford & Zhang, 1993). Technology-based distance education delivery modes vary according to the interaction they allow between instructor and learners, and distance learning methods that provide higher levels of interactivity often appear to be the most successful (Hackman & Walker, 1990). For purposes of illustration, it is helpful to consider a continuum of interactivity, with traditional campus classrooms at one end and very basic correspondence courses at the other.

Traditional campus classrooms allow instructor and student to interact most fully—during class, as well as before, after, and outside of class. Even larger "lecture hall" classes offer access to the instructor or teaching assistants. Students and instructors gather together regularly for live, "real time" class meetings. Classroom activities may include faculty-student discussions, question and answer periods, and other interactions. Often there is an opportunity for instructors to look "over the students' shoulder" when they are engaged in computer mastery, chemistry labs, and engineering projects. This interactivity is easily accomplished on traditional campuses.

At the other end of the continuum, *very basic* correspondence courses offer little or no opportunities for student-faculty interaction. Students enroll in a course, receive materials via mail, complete a required package of self-paced educational activities, and return their self-instructional materials for review or grading. In this basic arrangement, little student-instructor exchange exists and there is no opportunity for "over the shoulder" consultation. Other institutions with *contemporary* correspondence programs and independent study programs provide more extensive, well-developed student services that can include tutoring, career planning, academic advising, and other supports.

In between traditional campus classrooms and very basic correspondence courses, different technology-based distance learning modes provide opportunities for varied amounts, and types, of faculty-student interaction. The amount can be relatively high to relatively low. Using two-way interactive televised instruction, students and instructors may be able to see, hear, and communicate with one another during regular class meetings, via two-way microphones and video hook-ups. Using computer network-based instruction, students and instructors may be able to hold email conversations and chat room discussions.

Faculty-learner interaction can be *synchronous* or *asynchronous* (Ancis, 1996; Anderson, Benjamin, Busiel, & Paredes-Holt, 1998): For example, two-way electronic classroom interactions and chat room discussions are synchronous. This means there is no time-lag between each participant's contribution to the discussion. In other words, they take place in "real time" and are experienced by participants much like everyday, live, "real life" interpersonal interactions—more or less like a telephone conversation. In contrast, email and fax are asynchronous. This means they take place across a progressive sequence of separate communications by those involved, with a time-lag between each conversation segment. This is something like playing chess by mail. There are advantages to both synchronous and asynchronous interactions. Synchronous interactions feel more like a live conversation, are more spontaneous, and provide more immediate support. Asynchronous interactions allow participants to respond at their own convenience or according to their schedules and allow time for thought and reflection in-between responses.

Learner-Learner Interactivity

Learner-learner interactivity is another consideration in distance student satisfaction and success (Schwitzer & Lovell, 1999). For illustration purposes, it is helpful once again to consider a continuum of peer interactivity, with traditional campuses at one end and very basic forms of independent learning at the other end. On the traditional campus, there is opportunity for classroom support from other students as well as peer interactions that naturally occur in the campus social environment outside the classroom (in residence halls, student activities, dining halls, etc.). Even commuter students on traditional campuses have opportunities for a relatively high level of learner-learner interactivity. At the other end of the continuum, basic forms of independent learning that do not make use of information- and communications-technologies provide little or no opportunity for interaction with peer learners.

In between, distance education delivery modes differ according to the interactivity they allow between learners. Broadcast telecourses received in one's home do not provide a chance for student discussion, group projects, or peer consultation. Self-paced computer courses usually are not designed for high levels of peer interaction. On the other hand, learning activities in two-way interactive classrooms often include in-class "group" learning activities via audio-visual technologies, as well as peer interactions outside of class using fax and telephone (Barker & Platten, 1988; Bliner, Bink, Huffman, & Dean, 1995). Delivery systems that utilize Web-based learning, chat rooms, listserves, usenet newsgroups, electronic libraries, and other computer-driven methodology also usually produce productive environments for asynchronous or synchronous learner-learner interaction (Tagg, 1994).

Access to Support Services and Resources

Finally, distance education programs are definable by the access they provide to student services, supports, and other resources. Distance learning methods create obvious challenges for student affairs practitioners, including finding ways to deliver academic support and developmental programming, and to create community among learners who are geographically distant and widespread. Further, as traditional four-year institutions expand into distance learning, their distance student population will become more non-traditional and more similar to those who have historically enrolled in community colleges (Schwitzer, 1997a). Therefore, the most effective models of distance student service delivery usually borrow from community college models. At the same time, modes of delivery must be creative enough to overcome geographic and technological challenges (Schwitzer, 1997a).

Distance learners require such services as: an orientation focusing on the transition from the work world or community college to four-year college demands; technology training; career counseling, academic advising, and tutoring; assistance with time management, academic program planning, and goal setting; child care; and mentoring, support groups, and developmental counseling. Innovative modes of delivering student services include: videotaped orientation programs; telephone assistance and technology support; virtual office hours; on-line seminars designed to build community; and toll-free advising and counseling lines (Webster & Blair, 1997).

Traditional campuses tend to provide a full range of student services; and independent correspondence courses often provide only limited developmental support, although some independent learning programs build in more extensive student services. For their part, distance learning modes differ according to the access they provide to institutional services and resources ranging from comprehensive to minimal. Most comprehensively, some four-year institutions support their distance learner constituency through the use of geographically distant, satellite student affairs offices (perhaps located throughout a region at community college sites) (Ancis, 1996; Schwitzer, 1997a). Others utilize combinations of two-way audio-visual teleconferences, telephone, virtual office hours (using email or chat-rooms), or fax to provide services such as academic advising, orientation, and counseling (Peterson's Guides, 1998). Some intentionally create community through activities such as televised distance learner graduation ceremonies (Schwitzer, 1997a). On the other hand, because of varying institutional climates, concerns about cost-effectiveness, and technological challenges, some distance learning programs operate without providing much at all in the way of student services—or require distance learners to travel to an institution's main campus for needed services (Webster & Blair, 1998).

Modes of Delivery

In the preceding sections, we defined distance learning and discussed four characteristics associated with the electronic (or technologically-driven) delivery of contemporary American distance education: type of technology, faculty-learner interactivity, learner-learner interactivity, and access to support services and resources. This section presents the most common methods of electronically delivering distance education, including: (1) on-campus technology-assisted learning, (2) electronic college courses and on-line instruction, (3) broadcast television and teleclasses, and (4) interactive audio-video classes. We discuss the technology, faculty interactivity, peer interactivity, and access to services, associated with each of these distance education delivery modes. Table 1.1 summarizes the information presented in this section.

On-Campus Technology-Assisted Learning

Increasingly, on-campus learning is enhanced by the use of electronic technologies. Some technologies, such as high-tech classrooms and computer programs for making audio-visual presentations, are used to augment instruction *within* the classroom. These are examples of advanced electronic instructional methods, but they are not distance learning. On the other hand, when electronic technologies allow instructor and students to communicate in novel ways, or bring instructor and students together from disparate locations across (or near) campus, these approaches should be recognized as a type of distance learning application.

Most commonly, this takes the form of (a) faculty consultation and advising through e-mail or faculty Web pages, or (b) computer-assisted instruction offered through chat rooms and other forms of computer conferencing. Asynchronous communication occurs when faculty and students communicate through e-mail and link to various Web sites related to course topics. In contrast, computer conferencing allows for synchronous "group discussions" or "seminars" by connecting faculty and students together in a regional, nationwide, or worldwide computer network. This differs from e-mail approaches in that multiple messages are sent and read by participants simultaneously. Usually this approach emphasizes course- and institution-specific networking. However, some education experts already have suggested the possibility of a computerized national school system and other broad-based, multiple-institutional configurations based on computer-driven learning (Cummins & Sayers, 1996). These approaches enhance on-campus learning by allowing students to "plug in" to course discussions outside of class, anywhere a personal computer is located. When faculty accept class assignments (or at least first-drafts of class assignments) via fax or overnight mail, they also are utilizing basic distance learning methods to augment on-campus classroom teaching.

As seen in Table 1.1, on-campus courses that utilize technology-assisted alternatives require student access to computers in their residence hall or apartment, workplace or elsewhere; often result in increased interactivity among instructor and class members; and provide students with access to all of the institution's main campus services.

In addition, off-campus classes, in which faculty teach at nearby locations of convenience to local learners (for example, when an urban university offers courses in a suburb, away from its main campus), also should be considered a basic form of distance education. Local off-campus courses often rely on e-mail, computer conferences, telephone, and fax to supplement in-class interactions.

Electronic College Courses and Online Instruction

Electronic college courses are a form of true distance learning. They allow students who are geographically distant from an institution's main campus to complete specific college courses for academic credit. Often learners complete electronic college courses at their own pace. In the basic version of the electronic college course, students receive computer-packaged lessons and assignments, which are completed at home or in the workplace and returned to the institution electronically (using computer systems such as email or Websites) or through the mail. Faculty instructors evaluate the student's materials and return them with a midpoint or final grade or with directions for further work. Electronic courses delivered to the student in the form of pre-packaged computer programs often are enhanced or supplemented by pre-packaged audiotapes, videotapes, and printed material. For example, Chestnut Hill College (Philadelphia, PA) delivers graduate programs in its local area via computer packages supplemented by course videotapes, and Weber State University (Ogden, Utah) uses computer software, plus a combination of videotapes and audiotapes, to deliver undergraduate programs in accounting, anthropology, geology, political science, and other degrees to distance learners' homes (Peterson's Guides, 1998). The basic version of the electronic college course requires that students have easy computer access and adequate computer competency. This form of distance instruction involves low faculty-learner interactivity and little, if any, learner-learner interactivity. Support services are usually minimal, including only admissions counseling, financial aid counseling, and academic advising. Therefore, learners enrolling in basic electronic college courses are required to be self-motivated, independent learners, and self-directed.

World Wide Web-based or Internet-based classes are more advanced forms of the electronic college course. This format—referred to as *online instruction*—supplements (or sometimes replaces) home-delivered, prepackaged course materials with courses established on institutional Websites available on the Internet only to enrolled students. Instead of receiving a package of stand-alone instructional computer software and other materials through the mail, students enroll in a course, and then log on to an Internet Website that contains the class syllabus, readings, assignments, and the like. Further, instead of just independent work, all students in a course are usually required to "attend class" by logging on to Website discussions at designated class chat times. The instructor and students also utilize course-specific email and chat rooms for discussions outside of "class time". For example, New York University's Virtual College utilizes a combination of computer software and the World Wide Web to deliver graduate programs in business management and information technology (Peterson's Guides, 1998). Web-based courses allow for more instructor-learner and learner-learner interaction than prepackaged electronic courses alone.

The most advanced electronic college courses also rely on telecommunications technology to improve faculty-learner interactivity. Along with delivering courses by computer software and synchronous Web-based class meetings and chat times, advanced forms of electronic courses require students to communicate with instructors via telephone, mail, and fax. At Weber State University, like many other institutions, students and instructor interact via mail, telephone, and email. Some colleges and universities go further by providing periodic teleconferencing or requiring occasional student visits to the institution's main campus (Peterson's Guides, 1998).

In addition, the most advanced electronic college programs utilize computer networking and telecommunications to provide more comprehensive distance student support services. Common distance services include access to library resources, academic advising, career placement, and tutoring at a distance.

Broadcast Television and Teleclasses

Broadcast television courses are offered by community colleges, colleges, and universities through commercial or public T.V., and are broadcast or cable-delivered into students' homes. Telelearning Network Services at Delta College (University Center, MI), for example, offers Associate Degrees in General Studies and bachelors degrees in dozens of academic majors (Peterson's Guides, 1998). Broadcast television courses include live class-meetings or lectures that are shown during designated time-periods, as well as videotaped lectures that are shown repeatedly several times. Learners view the courses as they are broadcast, or may videotape them for later use. "Attendance" or videotape review is required.

This format relies on *one-way audio-video* to deliver distance education. Learners can see and hear the instructor, but the instructor cannot see or hear students. A few programs also incorporate telecommunications technology that allows students to telephone the instructor during class broadcasts in order to offer reactions and ask questions. This more advanced approach—which is similar to video-conferencing—utilizes *one-way video* and employs a simple form of *two-way audio*. While televised academic programs create a more accurate facsimile of the college classroom experience, they allow only minimal faculty-learner interaction (when telephones are used to provide two-way audio) and little or no learner-learner interaction. However, they provide more faculty-learner interaction than do electronic college courses, and they provide a visual interactive component not found in online instruction.

The *teleclass* format is similar to the broadcast television class, except that students in the course meet together in specially wired classrooms to view lectures by an instructor. These receptor classrooms may be located in corporate workplaces (or on military bases and ships), at local community college sites, or regional academic centers. The advantage of the teleclass format is that it allows students to interact with one another after watching live broadcasts or videotaped lectures. Sometimes a teaching assistant, proctor, or clinical instructor leads the discussion. The intended outcome of this format is to provide greater academic support and participant interaction.

Broadcast courses and teleclasses provide the focal learning experience associated with a college class at a distance. Commonly, they comprise the central component of a larger, more comprehensive distance instructional package. For example, Delta College's Telelearning Network broadcasts class lectures via television into students' homes, but also utilizes videotapes, videoconferencing, audiotapes, Web-based instruction, and print to deliver an entire college course (Peterson's Guides, 1998). The most common student services available to distance learners enrolled in broadcast and telecourses are academic advising, career placement assistance, library resources, and academic support which are accessed via telephone, email, and Internet connection.

Interactive Audio-Video Classrooms

The interactive audio-video classroom is the most technically advanced form of distance learning, although providing less flexibility in time and location for students. When this format is employed, the instructor conducts a "live" class from an actual main campus classroom with a group of main-campus students in attendance. Communications technology delivers the main campus class to multiple receptor classrooms at a number of geographically distant sites. The interactive classroom provides *one-way or two-way video interaction, and two way audio interaction,* between the main campus instructor and students at all the different classroom locations, and between the geographically separated students themselves.

Cameras, digital satellite, and video-monitors (or "televisions") deliver the visual presentation. *One way video* interaction occurs when the main campus picture is sent to all of the receptor classrooms simultaneously, but pictures of the distance classrooms are not sent back to the main campus instructor. Using *two-way video*, students everywhere can see the instructor, and students and the instructor can see students at all of the sites, as well. Microphones and wiring deliver the audio presentation. *Two-way audio* is always used, so that students everywhere can hear the professor, as well as students and the professor can hear students at all of the different sites.

There may be one or two distant classrooms across town, or dozens (or more) of simultaneous classes across the area, region, state, nation, or world. For example, Old Dominion University, simultaneously broadcasts interactive classes from its main campus in Norfolk, VA to dozens of receptor classrooms located on community college campuses across Virginia; to community college systems in partner states; to corporate centers near Washington, D.C. (so that employees can attend college conveniently, at work); and to military sites such as Quantico Marine

Base and designated Navy ships at sea. In turn, whether students are in the New River Valley, the Blue Ridge Mountains, or a suburb of Washington, D.C., small groups at each site combine to form one large electronic classroom of Old Dominion students (Oldenburg, 1996).

In the Old Dominion University illustration, *two-way audio and one-way video interaction* is usually employed. This means that students at all locations can *see and hear* the professor, they can *hear* everyone, and the professor also can *hear* students at all locations. Each student has his or her own microphone at his or her desk, and the sound is broadcast to all sites. In some classrooms, the video is also *two-way*; here, the professor views multiple distance sites on monitors, and can choose to allow everyone to view the participants at a given location.

Although interactive classrooms require student access to a distance academic center, they provide the most realistic facsimile of the traditional on-campus classroom learning experience. This format allows for higher faculty-learner interactivity and learner-learner interaction. Student affairs professionals sometimes are assigned to academic centers, community college campuses, and other sites, in order to provide in-person advising, counseling, career assistance, financial aid, and even student activities. The professor can use class discussion, group activities, demonstrations, debates, and other means to simultaneously engage both main campus students and distance learners who are attending the class electronically from one of the distance academic centers. Students can use class meetings for real interactions with peer learners and to complete group projects. As is true for other distance learning modes, learners enrolled in interactive classroom programs usually have access via telephone, email, and Internet to distance student services such as academic advising, library services, and academic support.

Why—and What—Should Student Development Professionals Know About Distance Learning?

Along with hardware, software, and transport, *trained professionals* are an essential component in distance education's telecommunications and information technology systems (Duning, Van Kekerix, & Zaborowski, 1993). Just as the role of teaching faculty remains essential amidst distance education's hard-wiring and software, there is an essential role for professionals who manage the system and support learners' and instructors' needs.

Distance learners need academic advising, career planning and management, counseling services, disability services, financial aid, learning assistance programs, multicultural student services, outcomes assessment and program evaluation, registrar services, and student orientation (Webster & Blair, 1998). Methods also are needed for creating a sense of community across geographic distances (Schwitzer, 1997). In turn, the electronic classroom challenges student affairs professionals to find innovative ways of delivering essential services. Institutions must develop support and service innovations that not only bridge geographic separation, but also meet the needs of changing constituencies. Student affairs practitioners are needed who can administer distance learning programs and design and manage the student services they require.

Distance education also requires greater emphasis on learner-centered teaching methods (Ancis, 1996; 1998). Distance learning instructors are changing how they teach in order to increase student involvement in learning—drawing on a combination of instructional models (LeBaron & Bragg, 1994), adult learning models (Wilkes & Burnham, 1991), and student development models (Coggins, 1988; Schwitzer & Lovell, 1999). In particular, they are moving toward active, engaging educational approaches that bring key college student development concepts into the electronic classroom (Schwitzer, 1997a).

The learner-centered approach emphasizes varied learning styles and recognizes student variables such as developmental differences, previous learning, gender and cultural differences, and motivational factors, so that classroom learning more closely matches student needs (Ancis, 1998). As a result, when campuses make the shift to learner-centered distance education, student affairs professionals, who are experts in learner-centered approaches, have the potential for greater involvement in distance academic life. Academic affairs, student affairs, and technical services must work collaboratively to meet the needs of learners in the electronic campus community.

References

Anderson, D., Benjamin, B., Busiel, C., & Parades-Holt, B. (1998). *Teaching online: Internet research, conversation, and composition (2nd edition)*. New York: Longman.

American College Personnel Association. (1994). *Student learning imperative: Implications for student affairs.* Washington, DC: Author.

American College Personnel Association (1996-present). *About Campus.* San Francisco: Jossey-Bass.

Ancis, J. R. (1998). Cultural competency training at a distance: Challenges and strategies. *Journal of Counseling and Development, 76,* 134-143.

Ancis, J. R. (1996, August). *Interactive-television and multimedia classrooms: Teaching psychology at a distance.* Symposium conducted at the annual meeting of the American Psychological Association, Toronto, Ontario, Canada.

Astin, A. W. (1985). *Achieving educational excellence.* San Francisco: Jossey-Bass.

Barker, B. O., & Platten, M. R. (1988). Student perceptions on the effectiveness of college credit courses taught via satellite. *The American Journal of Distance Education, 2,* 44-50.

Bennett, W. J. (1984). *To reclaim a legacy: A report on the humanities in higher education.* Washington, DC: National Endowment for the Humanities.

Beaudoin, M. (1990). The instructor's changing role in distance education. *The American Journal of Distance Education, 4,* 21-30.

Bishop, J. S. (1990). The university counseling center: An agenda for the 1990s. *Journal of Counseling and Development, 68,* 408-413.

Bliner, P. M., Bink, M. L., Huffman, M. L., & Dean, R. S. (1995). Personality characteristics differentiating and predicting the achievement of televised-course students and traditional-course students. *The American Journal of Distance Education, 9,* 46-60.

Bloland, P. A., Stamatakos, L. C., & Rogers, R. R. (1996). Redirecting the role of student affairs to focus on student learning. *Journal of College Student Development, 37,* 217-226.

Blyn, M. R., & Zoerner, C. E., Jr. (1982). The academic string pushers. *Change, 14,* 21-25.

Coggins, C. C. (1988). Preferred learning styles and their impact on completion of external degree programs. *The American Journal of Distance Education, 2,* 25-37.

Cummins, J., & Sayers, D. (1996). *Brave new schools: Challenging cultural illiteracy through global learning networks.* New York: St. Martin's.

Dillon, C. L., & Walsh, S. M. (1992). Faculty: The neglected resource in distance education. *The American Journal of Distance Education, 6*, 5-21.

Duning, B. S., Van Kerkerix, M. J., & Zaborowski, L. M. (1993). *Reaching learners through telecommunications.* San Francisco: Jossey-Bass.

Editorial Page Editors. (July 30, 1998). Long-distance learning: ODU leads nation: ODU courses are transmitted to the West Coast. *The Virginian-Pilot,* Norfolk, VA. p. B10.

Evans, T., & Nation, D. (1989). *Critical reflections on distance education.* Philadelphia, PA: Falmer Press.

Ewell, P. T., & Boyer, C. M. (1988). Acting out state-mandated assessment. *Change, 19*, 40-47.

Fulford, C. P., & Zhang, S. (1993). Perceptions of interaction: The critical predictor in distance education. *The American Journal of Distance Education, 7*, 8-21.

Ferguson, J. (1976). *The Open University from within.* London: University of London Press.

Garrison, D. R., & Shale, D. (1987). Mapping the boundaries of distance education: Problems in defining the field. *The American Journal of Distance Education, 1*, 7- 13.

Giddan, N. S., & Weiss, S. J. (1990). Costs and effectiveness of counseling center dropout prevention. *Journal of College Student Development, 31*, 100-107.

Guskin, A. (1997). Learning more, spending less. *About Campus, 2*, 4-9.

Hackman, M. Z., & Walker, K. B. (1990). Instructional communication in the televised classroom: The effects of system design and teacher immediacy on student learning and satisfaction. *Communication Education, 39*, 196-206.

Keegan, C. D. (1986). *The foundations of distance education.* London: Croom Helm.

Kozloff, J. (1987). A student-centered approach to accountability and assessment. *Journal of College Student Personnel, 28*, 419-424.

LeBaron, J. F., & Bragg, C. A. (1994). Practicing what we preach: Creating distance education models to prepare teachers for the twenty-first century. *The American Journal of Distance Education, 8*, 5-19.

Moore, M. G. (1988). Telecommunications, internationalism, and distance education. *The American Journal of Distance Education, 2,* 1-7.

Oldenburg, D. (April 2, 1996). Going the distance: Old Dominion's burgeoning electronic university program. *The Washington Post,* Washington, D.C. p. B5.

Osborne, J. L., & House, R. M. (1995). Evaluation of counselor education programs: A proposed plan. *Counselor Education and Supervision, 34,* 253-269.

Overbaugh, R.C. (1994). Research-based guidelines for computer-based instruction development. *Journal of Research on Computing in Education, 27,* 29-47.

Perry, W. (1977). *The Open University.* Washington, DC: Jossey-Bass.

Peters, O. (1971). Theoretical aspects of correspondence instruction. In O. McKenzie & E. Christen (Eds.). *The Changing World of Correspondence Study.* College Park, PA: The Pennsylvania State University.

Peterson's Guides. (1998). *The electronic university: A guide to distance learning.* Princeton, NJ: Peterson's Guides.

Reddy, G. R. (1988). (Ed.). *Open universities: The ivory towers thrown open.* New Dehli: Sterling Publishers.

Schwitzer, A. M. (1997a). Supporting student learning from a distance. *About Campus, 2,* 27-29.

Schwitzer, A. M. (1997b). Utilization-focused evaluation: Proposing a useful method of program evaluation for college counselors and student development professionals. *Measurement and Evaluation in Counseling and Development, 30,* 50-61.

Schwitzer, A. M. (1998). Applying the *Student Learning Imperative* to counseling center outcome evaluation. *Journal of College Student Psychotherapy, 13,* 71-92.

Schwitzer, A. M., & Lovell, C. (1999). Effects of goal instability, peer affiliation, and teacher support on distance learners. *Journal of College Student Development, 40, 43-53.*

Sorensen, A. (July 30, 1998). Long-distance learning: ODU leads nation: ODU courses are transmitted to the West Coast. *The Virginian-Pilot,* Norfolk, VA. p. B10.

Smith, P., & Kelly, M. (1987). *Distance education and the mainstream.* NY: Croom Helm.

Tagg, A. C. (1994). Leadership from within: Student moderation of computer conferences. *The American Journal of Distance Education, 8,* 40 48.

Tunstall, J. (1973). (Ed.). *The Open University opens.* London: Routledge & Kegan Paul.

Wagner, L. (1973). The economic implications. In J. Tunstall (Ed.). *The Open University opens* (pp. 21-27). London: Routledge & Kegan Paul.

Webster, C. E., & Blair, C. R. (1998, March). *Student services and programs in distance learning environments.* Paper presented at the annual meeting of the American College Personnel Association, St. Louis, MO.

Wilkes, C. W., & Burnham, B. R. (1991). Adult learner motivations and electronic distance education. *The American Journal of Distance Education, 5,* 43-50.

Wingspread Group on Higher Education. (1993). *An American imperative: Higher expectations for higher education.* Racine, WI: Johnson Foundation.

Wolcott, L. L. (1995). The distance teacher as reflective practitioner. *Educational Technology, Jan/Feb,* 39-43.

Zigerell, J. (1991). *The uses of television in American higher education.* New York: Praeger.

Chapter 2

Higher Education and Distance Learning in the United States: Knowledge Base and Practice

What have Big Bird and Cookie Monster got to do with distance learning and higher education in the United States? The answer is that "Sesame Street"—the children's T.V. series populated by these two characters and their friends, Bert and Ernie and the Grouch—was a watershed experience for instructional broadcasting in the United States. "Sesame Street", which originally aired in 1968, was the first endeavor to demonstrate that instructional broadcasting *works*—by showing that learning experiences could be efficiently delivered via telecommunications technology, received by a large population of constituent learners, and produce educational outcomes. It was in America's "post-Sesame Street" period that education via telecommunications first appeared to be *practical* (Zigarell, 1991).

Thirty years after Sesame Street's original broadcast, distance learning continues to be guided by the practical question, "What will work?". Combining whatever methods work, and using whatever division of labor and technology seems necessary, in order to mass produce and mass deliver higher education, defines the American *pragmatic eclectic approach*.

American Distance Learning: Pragmatic Eclecticism

American distance learning is an applied discipline that borrows from other fields to guide its practice (Cyrs, 1997). Distance educators apply a combination of organizational systems models, a variety of instructional models, adult learning models such as those that guide community college work, and various student affairs approaches to their educational and student development practice. This borrowing and combining of methods describes an *eclectic* approach.

Examples of eclecticism can be found throughout college student development. For example, when a division of student affairs borrows some principles to guide its practice from contemporary student development theories [such as Chickering (1969) or Perry (1970)], borrows some principles from the *in loco parentis* philosophy, and borrows still other guidelines from the *Student Learning Imperative* (ACPA 1994), the division is practicing student services eclectically. The result might be a division that simultaneously provides programs that help first-year students meet their everyday needs (i.e., *in loco parentis*), residence hall designs that promote autonomy and mature decision-making (i.e., applying student development theories), and health center services aimed at improved student knowledge and understanding of important health issues (i.e., *Student Learning Imperative*). Similarly, a career center staff is practicing eclectically when they combine individualized services, group programs, and self-directed career search approaches—and counseling centers work eclectically when they take a developmental approach that includes one-to-one counseling for some students, but offer a more psychiatric approach that includes medication to meet other students' needs.

Eclectic practice contrasts with practice that is organized and guided by one specific, unifying theoretical perspective (e.g., contemporary student development theory versus *in loco parentis*). When practice is derived from a singular theoretical approach, an advantage is that outcome goals, methods employed to obtain intended outcomes, and criteria used to measure outcomes are all determined by the model employed and the research that exists to back up the model. Such an approach determines which outcomes are theoretically desirable, and suggests a means for reaching them. On the other hand, when practicing eclectically, no single body of information exists from which to reliably and consistently determine exact outcome goals and effective methods of reaching those goals.

So far, there has been very little theory-driven, empirically-based research to establish and expand distance education's conceptual foundation. Rather, most data-based studies related to distance learning have been limited to the examination of program implementation and learner satisfaction (Saba & Shearer, 1994). The eclectic practice of distance learning primarily has been guided by *pragmatists,* who develop, implement, and modify new systems according to what is necessary to get a distance learning program up-and-running, through a series of "piecemeal modifications" (Perry, 1977, p. 1; Moore, 1993). Decision-making in the American form of distance learning is based on economic considerations, technological considerations, as well as pedagogical considerations. The bottom line is that distance learning approaches respond to public pressures for greater access and efficiency, using advancing technologies.

Pragmatic Eclecticism and the British Open University Model

Table 2.1 provides a comparison of the American model and its predecessor, the British Open University. The British Open University model of distance learning was developed to reach a specific constituency: working class learners who had limited access to traditional British institutions. The goal of the Open University approach is best described as the democratizing of higher education. The basic Open University model reached learners by using a specific approach: (a) publically broadcast television courses combined with (b) independent study. The Open University model has been adapted extensively worldwide (Smith & Kelly, 1987; Reddy, 1988). By comparison, American distance learning is best described as the industrialization of higher education—the mass production of teaching and learning using new cost-efficient and effective methods of delivery. The American approach reaches the widest, most eclectic audience possible wherever a demand is found and practically can be met. The American approach delivers new methods anywhere there is a demand.

Table 2.1

American Pragmatic Eclecticism and British Open University:
Comparing Two Distance Learning Models

	Model	
Characteristic	**American Model**	**British Open University**
Approximate Start-up	Mid-1980s	Early 1970s
Goal	Industrialize delivery of higher education[1]	Democratize access to higher education[2]
Objective	Use a new division of labor and technology to mass produce high-quality teaching and learning[1]	Mitigate social inequity by "opening up" college opportunities to educationally under-privileged groups[2]
Catalytic Forces	Political/Economic: Declining public support/ Calls for more efficient, learner-centered institutions	Political/Social: Pressures to reach out to "educationally under-privileged" constituency
Primary Delivery Methods	Telecommunications Information Technologies	Broadcast Television Correspondence
Constituent Benefits	Wider, less expensive access Access overcomes geography Flexibility for adult learners	Qualifier exams not required Access overcomes geography Flexibility for adult learners
Institutional Benefits	Reach wider constituency Increased revenue Enhanced public support	Effective method of reaching population in need

1. Keegan, C. D. (1986). *The foundations of distance education.* London: Croom Helm
2. Tunstall, J. (Ed.). (1973). *The Open University opens.* Amherst: University of Mass. Press

A Growing Knowledge-Base for Practice:
Major Themes in the Literature

Because the eclectic approach is not guided by a single, universally accepted, over-arching conceptual framework to determine what learning and development outcomes are theoretically desirable—and perhaps more importantly, how to specifically foster desired learning and student development—administrators, educators, and student development professionals at each institution must establish their own decision-making process about how to design, implement, and assess distance learning. A distance learning knowledge-base is developing out of these various efforts. The most important themes to emerge from the growing literature include: defining distance education, assessing student satisfaction, the relationship between student learning styles and personality characteristics and distance learning outcomes, and the relationship between interactivity and distance learning outcomes.

Defining the Field

Early writing on the topic of American distance education primarily focused on establishing the new discipline. The initial need in the literature was to "build a case" for distance learning and define its parameters. The challenge was to define and describe the concept of distance education in a way that was useful for the institutions that would be implementing it. An overly narrow concept of what was theoretically desirable for distance learning would be unlikely to describe what different institutions were actually *doing* day-to-day and therefore would not be practical; on the other hand, neither would an overly broad concept of distance education provide any meaningful parameters to guide every-day practice (Garrison & Shale, 1987; Keegan, 1986). In order to find a definitional middle ground, two initial questions were asked:

1) Is American distance education the same as open education (its predecessor)?
2) What is the relationship between distance and conventional forms of education?

The answer to the first question is that distance learning systems may be either open or not open (Keegan, 1986; 1988). Open learning systems (i.e., those that follow the British Open University model) always have the goal of democratizing access to higher education, and pursue this goal by using open enrollment requirements, employing educational materials that emphasize an openness to alternative learning styles, using open cut-off dates for assignments, and providing students with open access to administrators (Keegan, 1986; McKenzie, Postgate, & Scupham, 1975). Individual distance learning programs may or may not adopt any components of the open learning formula. Conceptually, they are "more open" to the degree that they adopt some or all of these components.

The answer to the second question has been debated. One perspective is that distance education is simply another mode of teaching (Moore, 1973). Therefore, as new information and communication technologies develop, distance teaching methods "will gradually merge with conventional forms of education so that the distinctions between the two become blurred" (Keegan, 1988, p. 5). In this case, distance learning is seen as one additional tool for providing higher education. Traditional teaching methods may be augmented or, in some cases, replaced by new technology-driven distance learning approaches. As a result, the two approaches are predicted to converge and meld as more institutions adopt distance systems (Smith & Kelly, 1987).

A competing perspective is that two distinct forms of higher education now exist: a dominant form, which is "conventional, oral, group-based" education, and a competing form, namely distance learning (Keegan, 1988, p. 5). Here, conventional, face-to-face teaching is seen as a method based firmly on direct interpersonal communication, whereas distance education is industrialized teaching based on technology (Keegan, 1986; Peters, 1973).

From the first perspective—the two instructional approaches are intersecting, converging educational tools that are different sides of the same coin—distance learning is always viewed positively. Distance learning is perceived as a definite asset, since it enhances higher education. From this perspective, the task facing faculty and student services staff is to understand the new methodology in the same way they would seek to understand other institutional practices, so that they have access to all of the available tools for effectively promoting college student learning and development.

From the second perspective—distance education and conventional forms of instruction are qualitatively different and competing systems—

distance learning is viewed neither positively or negatively *per se* (Keegan, 1988). Rather, conventional education may be seen as addressing its own design, implementation, and assessment questions while distance education deals separately with its process. Alternatively, distance education may be viewed as a new approach that is independent of the traditional approach but with its own valued purposes and methods; or distance education may be seen as a competing force. For example, at some institutions where there is a large, growing, and seemingly disproportionate investment in distance learners, distance education may be seen as the "tail" wagging the institutional "dog" to the neglect or compromise of main campus faculty, staff, and learners. According to the second perspective, the fundamental task facing administrators, faculty, and student services is to determine how institutional financial resources, faculty resources, and staff will be divided between the two competing enterprises, and toward what institutional goals. The task of understanding new methodologies then follows for those institutional personnel who are assigned the responsibility for implementing distance learning.

Regardless of the perspective taken, the fact remains that distance education introduces diverse, new options for delivering learning. As a result, the presence of distance delivery systems may fundamentally change the educational landscape, by having the effect of "privatizing" institutional learning (Keegan, 1986, p. 50). This means that as new and more options for pursuing higher education appear, the student/constituent/consumer may become the main force guiding the college marketplace, rather than institutions.

> Education as a public monopoly will cease to exist. The future for most institutions will be determined by the extent to which they have an educational product or products that are provided conveniently for the consumer at a competitive cost. (Cyrs, 1997, p. 9)

What exactly defines the practice of "distance learning"? According to the literature (Keegan, 1986; see Table 2.2), key elements of distance learning include: geographic separation between instructor and learners; the relative lack of a learner peer group; and use of electronic media and two-way communication to bridge the geographic gap and deliver course content.

Table 2.2
Theory into Practice: Definition of Distance Learning[1]

Distance learning is a form of education characterized by:

the semi-permanent separation of instructor and learner throughout the duration of the learning process

the active involvement of the institution in the planning and preparation of learning materials, and in the provision of student support services

the use of media and technologies to unite instructor and learner and deliver course content, including print, audio, video, or computer

the semi-permanent absence of a learning group or cohort through the duration of the learning process, so that people primarily learn individually and not in groups, except for the possibility of meetings for both didactic and socialization purposes

---

1. Keegan, D. (1986). *The foundations of distance education*. New York: St. Martins Press.

Use of technology *for two-way communication* distinguishes distance education from technology that is used only to augment instruction inside traditional classrooms. Also, institutions are often involved in the distance learner's educational process and provide adequate student support services. Although some institutions have provided a moderate range of student services for learners pursuing independent study, the university's ability to be more involved with distance learners and to provide more student services distinguishes distance learning from many basic independent study programs. As a foundation for practice, therefore: 1) institutional investment in the life of the distance learner is needed to promote students' learning and development; 2) instructional methods are needed that bridge the geographic separation between instructor and learners, and take full advantage of communications technology; and 3) student services are needed that fully support distance learners and build community at a distance. These are the subjects of the remaining chapters of this book.

Distance Learners: Perceptions, Attitudes, and Satisfaction

The next important theme in distance learning's formative literature is the assessment of student satisfaction. Studies evaluating distance learning programs typically have used descriptive methods to examine learner perceptions and attitudes (Saba & Shearer, 1994). Measuring student satisfaction is important to two stakeholder groups (Patton, 1988; Schwitzer, 1997a). First, administrators utilize student perception data to help "build the case" for distance learning viability, and to guide institutional decision-making about programs and resources. Administrators use student perception data for *instrumental* purposes driven by institutional needs (Holmberg, 1987).

Second, faculty and staff practitioners use satisfaction data as one measure of successful program implementation (Schwitzer, 1997a). For example, Ancis (1997) assessed the degree to which distance learning students pursuing a Bachelor's Degree in Human Services, compared to their main campus peers, were satisfied with their academic program across a number of dimensions. Seventy-six percent of distance students reported that they were either satisfied or very satisfied that the distance learning program increased their self-confidence in working with clients. Ninety-two percent of distance students reported that they were satisfied or very satisfied with the degree to which the program improved their knowledge of the human services profession. Eighty-two percent or distance students reported that they were satisfied or very satisfied that the degree program encouraged them to pursue the human services profession. Interestingly, no significant differences emerged between main-campus students and distance students on any measure of satisfaction.

While the success of a program ultimately must be measured by student performance and achievement, satisfaction is a critical *intermediate* outcome goal because achieving higher learner satisfaction is expected to produce higher levels of student motivation, greater commitment to the program, and in turn, better retention (Biner, Dean, & Mellinger, 1994). These intermediate factors are prerequisites to better learning, higher achievement, and successful program completion (Patton, 1988; Schwitzer, 1987), because students who express greater satisfaction with distance education are more likely to enroll in additional courses and programs (St. Pierre & Olsen, 1991). They also are more likely to recommend distance programs to others (Biner, et al., 1994).

For example, Barker and Platten (1988, p. 47) examined student satisfaction with two-way interactive televised instruction. In the descriptive study, nearly two-thirds of learners felt televised courses maintained their interest as well as (54%) or better than (8%) conventional classroom instruction—and similarly, just over two-thirds (69%) of participants reported they would enroll in subsequent distance classes. On the other hand, the remaining third said that televised classes were less interesting than traditional courses (38%), it was easier to "let their mind wander" (31%), and they would not be interested in future distance coursework (31%).

Several specific factors appear to underlie distance learner satisfaction (Biner, 1993; Biner, Dean, & Mellinger, 1994; St. Pierre & Olsen, 1991). These factors can be divided into two categories: a) those associated with instruction, and b) those related to student services.

Satisfaction with Instruction

Satisfaction with instruction is related to: 1) the instructor's teaching ability using distance methods, 2) the technical adequacy of the delivery system, and 3) access to the instructor for out-of-class communication. More specifically, learners experience greater satisfaction when the instructor is a good manager of the electronic class procedure (Biner, Dean, & Mellinger, 1994), actively engages students in the learning process rather than just lecturing on television (Cyrs, 1997), provides an opportunity for didactic conversation, and provides ongoing feedback to students about their progress (St. Pierre & Olsen, 1991). Further, students experience more satisfaction with instructional content when experiential learning is emphasized, and when they are able to apply knowledge meaningfully to their everyday life outside of the classroom (St. Pierre & Olsen, 1991).

In addition to the instructor's teaching approach, an important factor affecting learner experiences and perceptions is whether the technology employed results in clear audio and video delivery and good two-way communications mechanisms (Biner et al., 1994). Even excellent distance instructors are unlikely to overcome the negative effects of inadequate or poorly functioning technology.

Learners also have more positive experiences when they have adequate access to instructors outside of the electronic classroom (Biner et al., 1994; Dillon & Walsh, 1992; Fulford & Zhang, 1993). This includes faculty availability through telephone, email, and fax for advising and consultation, as well as having an efficient means of exchange between instructor and student for papers, exams, and other course materials.

Satisfaction with Student Services

Satisfaction with support services is related to: 1) attitudes of distance-site student services staff, 2) user-friendliness of course registration and enrollment processes, 3) accessibility of various student supports, and 4) promptness of material delivery. More specifically, learners experience greater satisfaction when on-site staff are "conscientious" (Biner, 1993; Biner et al., 1994, p.62) and when adequate opportunities exist for interacting with student services personnel (St. Pierre & Olsen, 1991). In fact, a students' level of interaction with staff is an important predictor of his or her satisfaction (Ancis, 1997). As follows, course registration and student services generally must meet students' needs and respond to students' life situations.

Another key variable affecting *distance* learner satisfaction—one that is not of concern for on-campus learners—is whether class materials and educational paperwork are sent and received promptly between the origination site and the student (Biner et al., 1994; St. Pierre & Olsen, 1991). Two systems for delivering material exists: direct exchange (via email, fax, regular U.S. mail, or private overnight express) between instructor and students, and indirect exchange. Indirect exchange requires that mail be delivered to and from sites by student support personnel located at each end of the transaction.

As we stated earlier, trained professionals are essential to the successful delivery of education through technology (Duning et al., 1993). Satisfaction data consistently support the importance of both instruction and student affairs in creating effective distance education programs.

Learning Outcomes: The Role of Student Differences

Understanding student perceptions and the factors influencing learner satisfaction serves a formative function in the literature, providing administrators with needed decision-making data and practitioners with important feedback about achieving the intermediate goals of successfully implementing a distance learning program and retaining those enrolled. However, theory-driven, empirically based research is needed to establish, confirm, and expand a conceptual foundation for distance education practice (Saba & Shearer, 1994). Research is needed that contributes to "the search for a theory than can guide practical work" (Holmberg, 1987, p.17). Taking a college student development perspective, researchers must consider the role of student variables such as learning styles and personality differences; the role of faculty and their teaching methods; and the role of student services in supporting learners generally and higher-risk learners specifically.

What part, then, do student differences play in distance learning outcomes? In what ways do student learning styles—that is, differences in thinking, emotion, and action-taking—influence how distance students interact with and respond to the learning situation (Coggins, 1988)? The effects of individual differences have been examined from two major perspectives: 1) Learning Styles, according to Myers-Briggs Types, and 2) Personality Characteristics, according to the 16 Personality Factors model.

Learning Styles and Myers Briggs Types

The Myers-Briggs Type Indicator (MBTI) is a measure of personality types along four dimensions (Jung, 1971; Myers & McCaulley, 1985). College student development professionals have used Myers-Briggs "types" extensively to understand organizational dynamics (such as how different worker "types" can complement each other in an office or department) and student functioning (such as how different student "types" relate to each other as roommates, interact in groups, and learn in different classroom arrangements). In particular, the four dimensions of the Myers-Briggs model are useful for understanding cognitive, affective, and behavioral differences in learning performance (Ehrman, 1990; Lawrence, 1984) and the pursuit and accomplishment of academic goals (Atman, 1988). Briefly, the four dimensions are:

1. *Extroversion versus Introversion:* This dimension relates to how people are energized and oriented. Extroverted people tend to derive energy from interactions with others, and their primary focus is on the outer world of people and events. Introverted people tend to derive energy from solitary activities, and their primary focus is on internal ideas.

2. *Sensing versus Intuition:* This dimension relates to how people take in information. Sensing people primarily focus on practical and factual data from the world around them, while Intuitive people primarily focus on multiple possibilities and meanings, theory, and innovation.
3. *Thinking versus Feeling:* This dimension relates to how people use information to make decisions and reach conclusions. Thinking people tend to use a rational, cause-and-effect approach, while Feeling people tend to use an approach that considers social and personal context.
4. *Judging versus Perceiving:* This dimension relates to how people approach the world and implement decisions about situations. Judging people prefer organization, structure, and closure, while Perceiving people prefer flexibility, autonomy, and openness.

In academic situations, the four dimensions relate to the following learning preferences (Lawrence, 1984, p. 12):

5. *Extroversion:* A preference for activity, discussion, and group work.
   Introversion: A preference for reading, internal processing, and working alone.
6. *Sensing:* A preference for step-by-step, careful, thorough preparation; observation of specifics; and memory of facts.
   Intuition: A preference for concepts and relationships, imagination, theory, and reading.
7. *Thinking:* A preference for logical organization and objective material.
   Feeling: A preference for learning through personal relationships.
8. *Judging:* A preference for steady, orderly, work and prescribed tasks.
   Perceiving: A preference for informal problem solving, discovery, and flexibility.

In the learner-centered climate of distance education, instructors must develop electronic classroom experiences that are effective in meeting the needs of a wide range of students. The major implication of Myers-

Briggs/learning style research for distance faculty is that the *most* effective teaching approaches will be those that combine methods associated with *various* learning style preferences. The four sets of preferences and corresponding sets of learning tendencies provide the following roadmap for developing student-responsive distance instruction (Ehrman, 1990; Ehrman & Oxford, 1989; Lawrence, 1984):

1. Extroverted individuals tend to respond best to group activities that involve dialogue, discussion, and cooperative work, whereas introverted individuals tend to respond best to lectures, independent complex verbal tasks, and other activities that do not require extensive interpersonal interaction.
2. Sensing individuals tend to respond best to structured, point-by-point syllabi, traditional curricula, learning facts, doing study drills, viewing media, self-instruction, and independent study, whereas intuitive individuals respond best to induction, discussion, reading, cramming, and a focus on concepts versus detailed homework or drills.
3. Thinking individuals respond best to instructor-directed classes, lecture, and factual memory tasks, whereas feeling individuals respond best to small group work, help sessions, simulations, and role-plays.
4. Judging individuals respond best to more formalized instruction, predictable routine, clear assignments, and traditional classroom methods, whereas perceiving individuals respond best to more independent, creative, and nontraditional methods.

The Myers-Briggs type preferences of distance learners also have implications for student services. Since distance learners must assume greater individual responsibility for their own learning, the most effective student supports will be those that combine services needed by different students to help them plan, pursue, and complete their academic goals. Atman (1988) examined relationships between Myers-Briggs type preferences and distance learners' orientation to goals and accomplishment of goals. Atman (1988) reported that distance students' preferences for 1) *extroversion*, 2) *intuition*, 3) *thinking*, and 4) *judging* were advantageous for planning, pursuing, and completing academic goals.

In the area of initial goal-planning, extroversion, intuition, thinking, and judging each were associated with an ability to recognize needs, opportunities, and obstacles. Further, intuition, thinking, and judging also were associated with goal-setting skills; and both thinking and judging were associated with an ability to organize. When planning academic pursuits, the ability to recognize one's needs, opportunities, and challenges; set goals; and then organize for action are strengths for distance learners.

In the area of pursuing plans, extroversion, intuition, thinking and judging were each associated with selecting a specific strategy, implementing a plan, and following through. Further, thinking and judging both were associated with goal completion. The ability to implement one's own plan and follow through to completion are obvious strengths for distance learners, who must be primarily self-driven, self-motivated, and self-supporting in pursuit of their goals.

Several recommendations for distance student services emerge from these findings. First, distance learning orientation programs will be most effective when they include a component that advises students about the non-academic skills they will need to plan, pursue, and complete distance education goals, and helps students understand their individual strengths and potential obstacles. Second, individualized services addressing multiple non-academic skills—such as identifying needs, setting goals, developing a strategy and organizing, or following through to completion—may be needed by different individuals. Third, Atman (1988) recommended that programs for distance students include a self-monitoring component that helps learners keep track of their progress.

Personality Characteristics

Understanding differences in preferred learning styles helps distance faculty develop instructional approaches that best meet diverse student needs. Likewise, understanding which learning style preferences seem to provide the best advantages (and obstacles) in the distance education setting helps student development professionals tailor services to promote distance learner success. Similarly, information about distance students' personality characteristics may be used to inform instructional approaches and student services.

Biner, Bink, Huffman, and Dean (1995) examined relationships between 16 different personality characteristics using the 16PF (Cattell, Eber, & Tatsouka, 1970), an established personality assessment instrument, and final course grades earned among 163 students (123 females and 40 males) enrolled in two-way interactive classes. In summary, Biner et al. (1995) found that greater academic success was related to two individual qualities: 1) *Self-sufficiency* and 2) *Expedient Disregard for Social Rules.*

Self-sufficiency refers to individual resourcefulness and the preference for making one's own decisions. Self-sufficient individuals, in contrast to more group-oriented people, are independent, resourceful, and prefer to make their own decisions. Because distance learners have less access to institutional supports, must work more independently, and usually have access to only a few peers at their geographically remote classroom sites, it is not unexpected that more self-sufficient individuals would perform better than more group-oriented individuals who tend to rely on interpersonal relationships to guide their decisions, actions, and performance.

Disregard of Social Rules refers to a more self-indulgent, careless disregard for social and other rules. In contrast to individuals who are more conscientious, compulsive, and socially-precise, individuals who disregard social rules tend to be undisciplined in the face of institutional rules. A combination of factors may account for the seemingly counter-intuitive relationship between an expedient disregard for social rules and academic success. Because distance learners tend to be older students who are juggling family, job, and other mature responsibilities along with their college pursuits, higher levels of expedience and less regard for established norms and rules probably aid distance learners in "functionally adapting to the diversity of their responsibilities" (Biner et al., 1995, p. 57). Non-traditional distance learners may believe that making practical choices that attend to personal needs more than established institutional rules is necessary to manage hectic lives with competing time demands. They also may feel entitled as consumers—"paying customers"—to have more individualized choices and personal freedom in their academics.

An implication of these findings is that distance learners who are less self-sufficient may require more intensive and varied student services to be successful. Further, paradoxically, faculty and staff may also find that the most successful students are those individuals most often attempting to circumvent stated rules and guidelines in and outside of the electronic classroom. Some institutional systems and requirements may need to be more flexible, while at the same time, special efforts may be required to ensure academic rigor and the maintenance of a program's integrity. Faculty and student affairs staff may need to provide more individualized attention, spend more time with "special situations", and devote more professional energy to specific student concerns as they arise.

Learning Outcomes: The Changing Role of Faculty

Distance learning faculty tend to be permanent full-time tenure-track or tenured faculty in liberal arts and sciences (e.g., arts, humanities, social science, natural science) and professional fields (e.g., business, education, engineering, human services) who hold various ranks (assistant, associate, and full professors) and have been at their institutions for a substantial time-period (the mean ranges in different studies from 6 to 14 or more years) (Clark, Soliman, & Sungaila, 1985; Dillon, 1989; Dillon, et al., 1991; LaRose, 1986). They tend to be, experienced faculty who are broadening their teaching repertoire to meet institutional needs. While most distance learning research has focused on the learner (Beaudion, 1990), understanding distance teaching, and how faculty make the transition from conventional instruction, are important issues.

Distance Teaching

Myths associated with distance education and its reliance on technology include the following: Distance education is impersonal, the learning that occurs is perfunctory and lacks depth, and there is minimal need for faculty in the process (Beaudoin, 1990). In reality, very little distance education is done "just by lecturing on T.V.". Instead, distance faculty rely heavily on *student-centered, active learning* approaches that engage students in the learning process (Beaudoin, 1990; Dillon & Walsh, 1992; Peterson & Knapp, 1993). They use varied, active teaching methods, shortening lecture presentations and increasing discussions and practical exercises that focus on the meaningfulness of course material to learners' everyday professional and personal lives (Schwitzer, 1997b). Student involvement in learning is the foundation of distance learning approaches (Smith, 1991).

Faculty report that distance teaching requires personalized, empathic, engaged interactions with distance students both during class and in printed or electronic materials used outside of class (Dillon, 1989; Johnson &

Silvernail, 1990; Parer, 1988). For example, in a study of 102 students at 15 distance sites, Hackman and Walker (1990, p. 197) found that during class, learning increases when teaching includes more "immediacy behaviors" such as giving ongoing feedback and using appropriate vocal qualities to convey a connection between instructor and students. The learner-centered approach emphasizes varied learning styles and recognizes student variables such as developmental differences, previous learning, gender and cultural differences, and motivation, so that distance classroom teaching more closely matches a wider range of student needs (Schwitzer, 1997b).

Distance faculty also take advantage of electronic communications (such as e-mail, computer conferencing, resource distribution lists, electronic bibliographies, remote files) when they design their courses in order to increase faculty-learner and learner-learner "in-class", "outside of class", and "homework" interactions. Because some methods (like e-mail) allow asynchronous communications and others (like computer conferencing) are synchronous, students have a chance to sometimes reflect before responding or offering opinions, and sometimes engage in immediate electronic discussion, debate, or collaboration. In fact, as a result of the combined opportunities for faculty-learner interaction during class and electronically, some research suggests that distance learners may be *more likely* than on-campus students to develop a productive one-on-one relationship with an instructor (Beaudoin, 1990). Distance faculty might use any of the following electronic communications activities shown in Table 2.3.

Table 2.3
Electronic Communication Activities[1]

The following electronic communication
activities can be used to increase interaction:

Case studies	Simulations
Cooperative learning	Guest "lectures" on line
Electronic field exchanges	On-line student services
Role plays	On-line library
Peer conferencing	On-line database searches

---

1. LeBaron, J. F., and Bragg, C. A. (1994). Practicing what we preach: Creating distance education models to prepare teachers for the twenty-first century. *The American Journal of Distance Education, 8,* (1) 5–19.

Making the Teaching Transition

Faculty who teach at a distance must alter their traditional instructional roles (Dillon & Walsh, 1992; Holmberg, 1986). In general, faculty who teach at a distance are positive about distance teaching (Dillon, 1989; Johnson & Silvernail, 1990; Taylor & White, 1991), and become more positive as they gain increased experience with distance teaching methods and technologies (Gilcher & Johnstone, 1989; Kirby & Garrison, 1989). However, faculty tend to be successful in modifying conventional teaching and gaining new distance teaching skills only when certain institutional conditions are in place.

The first condition is adequate professional development and training. Pre-service and ongoing in-service opportunities must both exist. Most faculty moving from traditional teaching on-campus to distance formats require two types of professional development. First, they need to understand how to use the required technology and distance format. For example, when interactive technology is used, training should include the use of two-way technology and interactive strategies; when prerecorded telecourses are used, training should focus on organizing materials, developing interactive study guides, and assessing student learning (Cyrs, 1989). Second, faculty must learn new teaching skills that will personalize the learning and incorporate student involvement strategies into the instructional experience (Dillon & Walsh, 1992; Smith, 1991). Training topics may include methods to establish and maintain effective communication between teacher and students and increasing interaction among students; strategies for encouraging individual and group motivation to learn at a distance; planning and managing organizational details, and developing an awareness of the time demands of distance delivered courses; and techniques for adding visual components to courses (Office of Technology Assessment, 1989, p. 95).

The second condition for the successful modification of conventional teaching and the development of new distance teaching skills is adequate institutional support. Institutional support involves removing institutional barriers to distance teaching success. Faculty have identified a variety of institutional barriers, including inadequate rewards and incentives; additional workload and lack of time; reduced student interaction and less spontaneity; and problems caused by technical failures, poor audio quality, and glitches in distribution of course materials (Dillon, Hengst, & Zoller, 1991; Johnson & Silvernail, 1990; McNeil, 1988; Taylor & White, 1991).

A main ingredient in institutional support is a "commitment from all levels, especially top administration, to overcome resource limitations, remove structural constraints, and combat attitudinal barriers" (Beaudoin, 1990, p. 27). Often times discrepancies exist between faculty's and administrators' perceptions of institutional support. Dillon (1989) found that while faculty at several institutions offering distance programs believed institutional enrollment and evaluation policies did not provide equitable reward for distance teaching, chief administrators at those institutions believed faculty teaching distance courses were adequately rewarded. When institutional support is low, technical problems exist, and training opportunities are inadequate, faculty tend to resist distance education, typically view it as a negative experience, and discontinue distance teaching. In contrast, when institutional support is high, evaluation and reward systems are equitable, and adequate professional development is provided, distance education attracts and retains high-quality faculty who make successful transitions to distance teaching.

Interactivity: The Key Variable?

One question is raised so often when discussing student differences and faculty roles that it deserves separate attention in our review of the literature, "Exactly how important is 'interactivity'? Is it the key variable for successful distance education?". As we noted above in our discussion of distance teaching, distance educators believe that interactivity, or personalized interactions, is centrally important to successful teaching and learning in electronic formats. Consistently, researchers examining the role of interactivity in distance learning have reported that personal interactions with faculty (Ancis, 1997, 1998; Fulford & Zhang, 1993), a "personalized empathic rapport with students" (Dillon & Walsh, 1992, p. 13), and faculty use of behaviors such as individualized student feedback and expressions of support (Hackman & Walker, 1990) are critical factors associated with distance learner satisfaction, persistence, and academic success—for televised distance learning as well as on-line courses (Wagner, 1997).

At the same time, a few researchers have reported that no relationship exists between interactivity and student retention and success (Coggins, 1988; Pugliese, 1994). In fact, as we noted earlier in our discussion of student personality differences, other research has shown that persistence and achievement among distance learners are related to individual learner "self-sufficiency" rather than a "group orientation" (Biner, Bink, Huffman, & Dean, 1995, p. 56)—or, "internal" rather than "external locus of control" (Dille & Mezack, 1991, p. 29) and more positive self-attitudes rather than psychosocial learning conditions (Coggins, 1988).

What is the more critical factor, student self-reliance or interactivity? What approach is more important for faculty and student services to adopt, fostering student self-reliance or trying to maximize supportive interactions? Two concepts help provide the answer:

1. Personal interaction versus Overall interaction;
2. Teacher Support versus Peer Affiliation.

Personal and Overall Interaction

"Personal interaction" refers to a student's perception of his or her own involvement with the instructor or other class members. An individual's perceptions of personal interaction in the electronic classroom comprises beliefs about: how often the person himself or herself answered questions asked by the instructor, volunteered an opinion, asked a question, and participated in overall class activities.

In comparison, "overall interaction" refers to a student's perceptions regarding interactions in the class generally, rather than one's own involvement. This includes the level of interaction between the instructor and other class members, the amount of class time devoted to instructor/student interactions, and the degree to which the instructor is perceived as motivating.

Fulford and Zhang (1993) examined the perceptions and satisfaction of 123 distance learners taking interactive audio/video televised classes. Interestingly, and perhaps contrary to what we might have expected, they found that while perception of *overall interaction* was a strong, significant predictor of a student's satisfaction with the distance classroom experience, the student's perceptions of *personal interaction* were only minimally useful for predicting their satisfaction levels. In fact, the students' impressions of the class' *overall interaction* level accounted for three times as much statistical variance in satisfaction as did impressions of *personal interaction*. Students' distance learning experiences seem to be more influenced by the overall interactivity they see and hear in class than by their own personal involvements in those interactions. Thus, research suggests that developing positive, successful overall group dynamics is more important to students' learning than trying too hard to engage every individual equally or to draw individual responses from each student.

Teacher Support and Peer Affiliation

Fulford and Zhang (1993) found that a more positive, interactive, comfortable *overall* psycho-social environment promoted better student experiences in distance classes. Previous research with on-campus groups similarly found that regardless of students' self-sufficiency, they prefer more interactive, engaging, supportive class settings (Robbins & Patton, 1985; Robinson & Cooper, 1988; Scott & Robbins, 1985; Schwitzer, Robbins, & McGovern, 1993).

Going a step further, two different components of overall classroom interactivity deserve consideration. "Teacher Support" is the extent to which the learner sees an instructor as interacting with, and expressing a personal interest in, students; whereas "Peer Affiliation" is the extent to which the learners view class members themselves as working together and becoming acquainted (Schwitzer & Lovell, in press; Tricket & Moos, 1973).

Schwitzer and Lovell (in press) examined the importance of teacher support and peer affiliation—along with the importance of self-sufficiency—for 79 students enrolled in interactive televised classes. As in previous studies, they found *Peer Affiliation* was a critical factor in distance learning experiences. When there was greater interactivity among class members, students reported greater general satisfaction, said the quality of learning was higher, and found classes more efficient.

On the other hand, when Schwitzer and Lovell (in press) examined the importance of *Teacher Support*, the results were more complicated. Teacher support influenced some students' experiences but not others. Specifically, among *more self-sufficient* learners, experiences were about the same regardless of teacher support; however, those demonstrating *less self-sufficiency* had better learning experiences when they perceived higher levels of support and involvement from the course instructor than when they did not perceive high levels of faculty involvement.

In other words, while all participants reported that greater interactivity among class members provided more opportunities for learning and development (general satisfaction), had more impact on the amount and nature of what they learned (quality of learning), and resulted in a more effective class experience (efficiency), less self-reliant participants tended to also rely on faculty interest and involvement for positive experiences. This was the case even when participants engaged in group learning activities in which the emphasis was on relationships with other learners rather than on interactions with the instructor.

In summary, while *self-sufficiency* is important to a student's pursuit and achievement of college educational goals when geographically separated from the supportive atmosphere of an institution's main campus, an *overall interactive classroom* environment or *overall interactive online* environment (Wagner, 1997) that provides opportunities for distance students to engage the instructor and one another allows for better learning experiences. Interactivity in televised classrooms and online courses allows instructors to increase participation and engage learners; develop communication by facilitating information-sharing and opinion-sharing; and enhance learning by allowing learners to practice with, and elaborate on, new learning (Wagner, 1994; 1997). Further, sources of *social support* such as peer affiliation, personalized faculty interactions, and relationships with student services seem to be necessary to the college pursuits of less self-sufficient individuals.

The Role of Student Services: Where Does Student Development Fit In?

This chapter provided a conceptual foundation for distance learning practice. The eclectic pragmatic approach involves discovering new ways to best meet learner and faculty needs. This means creating high-quality services and innovative methods that foster student satisfaction, since satisfaction is critical to adjustment and retention, and finding creative ways to promote learning and development, which are educational end-goals. Satisfaction requires responsive teaching, reliable technology, and engaging, interactive student services. Some student development practices, such as increasing the learner's interactions with peers, instructors, and student services, will be valuable for all students. For example, increasingly, student affairs professionals will use new communication and information technologies to interact with distance learners in order to: increase learners' connectedness with the institution and participation in learning; allow distance learners to express themselves; provide feedback; use institutional resources for academic and personal exploration and discovery; and bring closure at the end of their distance learning experience (Wagner, 1994; 1997). Other efforts will be more beneficial for higher-risk students, such as learners who are not natural organizers, goal-setters, or who are less self-directed. For example, student affairs professionals will interact with some distance learners to: help learners manage their overall program of study, and increase and maintain motivation (Wagner, 1994; 1997). Student affairs professionals also will work more closely with distance faculty and academic programs to achieve an institution's distance learning goals. By putting knowledge into practice, student affairs professionals have the opportunity to become even more involved in the technological, academic, and community life of their institutions through distance education. The changing role of distance student affairs practice is discussed in the following section.

References

American College Personnel Association (1994). *Student learning imperative: Implications for student affairs*. Washington, DC: Author.

Ancis, J. R. (1997). *TELETECHNET assessment report: Human services counseling program*. Norfolk, VA: Old Dominion University, Department of Educational Leadership and Counseling.

Atman, K. S. (1987). The role of conation (striving) in the distance education enterprise. *The American Journal of Distance Education, 1,* (1) 14-24.

Atman, K. S. (1988). Psychological type elements and goal accomplishment style: Implications for distance education. *The American Journal of Distance Education, 2,* (3) 36-44.

Barker, B. O., & Platten, M. R. (1988). Student perceptions on the effectiveness of college credits courses taught via satellite. *The American Journal of Distance Education, 2,* (2) 44-50.

Beaudoin, M. (1990). The instructor's changing role in distance education. *The American Journal of Distance Education, 4,* (2) 21-30.

Biner, P. M. (1993). The development of an instrument to measure student attitudes toward televised courses. *The American Journal of Distance Education, 7,* (1) 62-73.

Biner, P. M., Dean, R. S., & Mellinger, A. E. (1994). Factors underlying distance learner satisfaction with televised college-level courses. *The American Journal of Distance Education, 8,* (1) 60-71.

Biner, P. M., Bink, M. L., Huffman, M. L., & Dean, R. S. (1995). Personality characteristics differentiating and predicting the achievement of televised-course students and traditional-course students. *The American Journal of Distance Education, 9,* (2) 46-60.

Cattell, R. B., Eber, H. W., & Tatsuoka, M. M. (1970). *Handbook for the 16PF.* Champaign, IL: Institute for Personality and Ability Testing.

Chickering, A. (1969). *Education and identity.* San Francisco: Jossey-Bass.

Clark, R. G., Soliman, M. B., & Sungaila, H. (1985). Staff perceptions of external versus internal teaching and staff development. *Distance Education, 5,* 84-92.

Coggins, C. C. (1988). Preferred learning styles and their impact on completion of external degree programs. *The American Journal of Distance Education, 2,* 25-37.

Cyrs, T. E. (1989). *Designing a teleclass instructor's workshop addressing the differential skills needed for quality teleclass teaching.* Paper presented at the Fifth Annual Conference on Teaching at a Distance, Madison, WI

Cyrs, T. E. (Ed.). (1997). *Teaching and learning at a distance: What it takes to effectively design, deliver, and evaluate programs.* San Francisco: Jossey-Bass.

Dille, B., & Mezack, M. (1991). Identifying predictors of high risk among community college telecourse students. *The American Journal of Distance Education, 5,* 25-35.

Dillon, C. (1989). Faculty rewards and instructional telecommunications: A view from the telecourse faculty. *The American Journal of Distance Education, 3,* (2) 35-43.

Dillon, C., Hengst, H., & Zoller, D. (1991). Instructional strategies and student involvement in distance education: A study of the Oklahoma Televised Instruction System. *Journal of Distance Education, 6,* (1) 28-41.

Dillon, C. L., & Walsh, S. M. (1992). Faculty: The neglected resource in distance education. *The American Journal of Distance Education, 6,* (3) 5 -21.

Duning, B. S., Van Kerkerix, M. J., & Zaborowski, L. M. (1993). *Reaching learners through telecommunications.* San Francisco: Jossey-Bass.

Ehrman, M. E., & Oxford, R. L. (1989). Effects of sex differences, career choice, and psychological type on adult language learning strategies. *Modern Language Journal, 73,* 1-13.

Ehrman, M. E. (1990). The role of personality type in adult language learning: An ongoing investigation. In T. Parry & C. W. Stansfield (eds.), *Language aptitude: Past, present, and future research.* Englewood Cliffs, NJ: Prentice-Hall.

Fulford, C. P., & Zhang, S. (1993). Perceptions of interaction: The critical predictor in distance education. *The American Journal of Distance Education, 7,* (3) 9-21.

Garrison, D. R., & Shale, D. (1987). Mapping the boundaries of distance education: Problems in defining the field. *The American Journal of Distance Education, 1,* (1) 7-13.

Gilcher, K., & Johnstone, S. (1989). *A critical review of the use of audiographic conferencing systems by selected educational institutions.* College Park, MD: International Universities Consortium, University of Maryland.

Hackman, M. Z., & Walker, K. B. (1990). Instructional communication in the televised classroom: The effects of systems design and teacher immediacy on student learning and satisfaction. *Communication Education, 39,* (3) 196-206.

Hilgard, E. R. (1980). The trilogy of mind: Cognition, affection, and conation. *Journal of the History of the Behavioral Sciences, 16,* 107-117.

Holmberg, B. (1986). *Growth and structure of distance education.* London: Croom Helm.

Holmberg, B. (1987). The development of distance education research. *The American Journal of Distance Education, 1,* (3) 16-23.

Johnson, J. L., & Silvernail, D. L. (1990). *Report of faculty perceptions of Community College of Maine Instructional Television System, Fall 1989.* Augusta, Maine: University of Southern Maine.

Jung, C. G. (1971). *Psychological Types.* (H. G. Baynes, Trans.). Princeton, NJ: Princeton University Press.

Keegan, D. (1986). *Foundations of distance education* (1st ed.). London: Croom Helm.

Keegan, D. (1988). Problems in defining the field of distance education. *The American Journal of Distance Education, 2,* (2) 4-11.

Keegan, D. (1990a). *Foundations of distance education* (2nd ed.). NY: Routledge.

Keegan, D. (1990b). A theory for distance education. In M. G. Moore (ed.), *Contemporary Issues in American Distance Education* (pp. 327-332). Oxford, UK: Pergammon Press.

Kirby, D. M., & Garrison, D. R. (1989). *Graduate distance education: A study of the aims and delivery systems*. Paper presented at the Eighth Annual Conference of the Canadian Association for the Study of Adult Education, Cornwall, Ontario.

LaRose, R (1986). *Adoption of telecourses: The adoption and utilization of Annenberg/CPB Project telecourses*. Washington, DC: Annenberg/CPB Project.

Lawrence, G. (1984). A synthesis of learning style research involving the MBTI. *Journal of Psychological Type, 8,* 2-15.

LeBaron, J. F., & Bragg, C. A. (1994). Practicing what we preach: Creating distance education models to prepare teachers for the twenty-first century. *The American Journal of Distance Education, 8,* 5-19.

McKenzie, O., Postgate, R., & Scupham, J. (Eds.). (1975). *Open learning*. Paris: UNESCO.

McNeil, D. R. (1988). *Status of technology in higher education: A reassessment*. Paper presented at the Second Annual Conference on Interactive Technology and Communications, University of Maine at Augusta.

Myers, I. B., & McCaulley, M. H. (1985). *Manual: A guide to the development and use of the Myers-Briggs Type Indicator*. Palo Alto, CA: Consulting Psychologists Press.

Moore, M. (1973). Toward a theory of independent learning and teaching. *Journal of Higher Education, 44,* 661-679.

Moore, M. G. (1993). Is teaching like flying? A total systems view of distance education. *The American Journal of Distance Education, 7,* (1) 1-10.

Office of Technology Assessment. (1989). *Linking for learning: A new course for education*. Washington, DC: U.S. Government Printing Office.

Parer, M. S. (1988). *Institutional Support and Rewards for Academic Staff Involved in Distance Education*. Victoria, Australia: Centre for Distance Learning, Gippsland Institute.

Patton, M. Q. (1986). *Utilization-focused evaluation* (2nd ed.). Beverly Hills, CA: Sage.

Perry, W. G., Jr. (1970). *Forms of intellectual and ethical development in the college years*. New York: Holt, Rhinehart, & Winston.

Perry, W. (1977). *The open university.* San Francisco: Jossey-Bass.

Peters, O. (1973). Theoretical aspects of correspondence instruction. In O. McKenzie & E. Christensen (Eds.), *The changing world of correspondence study.* University Park: The Pennsylvania State University.

Peterson, P. L., & Knapp, N. F. (1993). Inventing and reinventing ideas: Constructivist teaching and learning in mathematics. In G. Cawelti (ed.). *Challenges and achievements of American education: The 1993 ASCD yearbook*, pp. 134-157. Alexandria, VA: Association for Supervision and Curriculum Development.

Pugliese, R. R. (1994). Telecourse persistence and psychological variables. *The American Journal of Distance Education, 8,* 22-39.

Reddy, G. R. (1988). *Open universities: The ivory towers thrown open.* New Dehli, India: Sterling Publishers.

Robbins, S. B., & Patton, M. (1985). Self-psychology and career development: Construction of the superiority and goal instability scales. *Journal of Counseling Psychology, 32,* 221-231.

Robinson, D., & Cooper, S. (1988). The relationship of Kohut's Self Psychology to career choice certainty and satisfaction. *Journal of College Student Development, 29,* 228-232.

Saba, F., & Shearer, R. L. (1994). Verifying key theoretical concepts in a dynamic model of distance education. *The American Journal of Distance Education, 8,* 36-59.

Schwitzer, A. (1997a). Utilization-focused evaluation: Proposing a useful method of program evaluation for college counselors and student development professionals. *Measurement and Evaluation in Counseling and Development, 30,* 50-61.

Schwitzer, A. (1997b). Supporting student learning from a distance. *About Campus* (July-August), 27-29.

Schwitzer, A. M., & Lovell, C. (In press). Effects of goal instability, peer affiliation, and teacher support on distance learners. *Journal of College Student Development.*

Schwitzer, A. M., Robbins, S. B., & McGovern, T. V. (1993). Influences of goal instability and social support on college adjustment. *Journal of College Student Development, 34,* 21-25.

Scott, K., & Robbins, S. B. (1985). Goal instability: Implications for academic performance among students in learning skills courses. *Journal of College Student Personnel, 23,* 378-383.

Smith, P., & Kelly, M. (Eds.). (1987). *Distance education and the mainstream: Convergence in education.* London: Croom Helm.

Smith, F. A. (1991). *Interactive instructional strategies: Ways to enhance learning by television.* Paper presented at the Seventh Annual Conference on Distance Teaching and Learning. Madison, WI.

St. Pierre, S., & Olsen, L. K. (1991). Student perspectives on the effectiveness of correspondence instruction. *The American Journal of Distance Education, 5,* (3) 65-71.

Taylor, J. C., & White, V. J. (1991). Faculty attitudes toward teaching in the distance education mode: An exploratory investigation. *Research in Distance Education, 3,* (3) 7-11.

Tricket, E. J., & Moos, R. H. (1973). Social environment of junior high and high school classrooms. *Journal of Educational Psychology, 65,* 92-102.

Tunstall, J. (1973). (Ed.). *The Open University opens.* London: Routledge & Kegan Paul.

Wagner, E. D. (1994). In support of a function definition of interaction. *The American Journal of Distance Education, 8,* 6–29.

Wagner, E. D. (1997). Interactivity: From agents to outcomes. In T. E. Cyrs (ed.), *Teaching and learning at a distance: What it takes to effectively design, deliver, and evaluate programs,* (pp. 19–26). San Francisco: Jossey-Bass.

Zigerell, J. (1991). *The uses of television in American higher education.* New York: Praeger.

Part II

Student Development at a Distance

P art II discusses student development concepts in the context of distance learning. This section builds on the distance education knowledge-base introduced in Part I by exploring distance student services which promote college adjustment, learning, and student development. Part II focuses on the role of student affairs professionals and supportive faculty as key resources who are critical to distance learner success. Thus far, the distance learning literature has tended to focus on the technology required to deliver higher education to new constituencies. There has been less focus on resources required by distance learners in order to support their academic goals. Chapter 3 describes distance learner characteristics and their student development needs. Chapter 4 discusses student affairs practices for providing services and creating community at a distance. Chapter 5 examines student affairs roles as educators who are critical to distance instruction. A case illustration follows, showing how student support is provided in one institution's distance program.

Chapter 3

Distance Learners: Characteristics and Needs

Student development professionals have led the way in understanding and responding to the growing diversity of American college campuses. This tradition is perhaps no more valuable than when it is directed to distance education because American distance learners are a varied, wide-ranging group (Pugliese, 1994; Wilkes & Burnham, 1991). Increasingly, college student personnel administrators are being asked to apply their know-how and expertise to the challenges of: understanding an institution's diverse distance learners, determining their learning and developmental needs, and then finding creative methods to meet those needs.

Because the specific goal of international models is to provide socially disadvantaged working-class learners access to higher education, most distance educators internationally work with a relatively limited, definable target population. In contrast, the American approach to distance education is to increase college access *wherever* a new, interested consumer constituency can be found, resulting in a demographically diverse student body. Here is a good illustration:

Aside from occasionally having to leave class to fly F-14's over the Persian Gulf, students in a new graduate accounting course . . . had a pretty normal semester.

All of them are sailors and pilots aboard the U.S.S. George Washington, a nuclear-powered air-craft carrier. They met every Sunday for four hours in a classroom beneath the flight deck. A two-way video signal allowed . . . their professors to give lectures, use visual aids, and answer questions almost as if they were right on the carrier instead of back on . . . campus. Outside of class, the students worked together in groups and communicated with their professors through electronic mail.

The on-board accounting course is one of three taught . . . since the ship left Norfolk last August. In all, the university has offered sailors 10 credits toward M.B.A. degrees . . .

The project required technicians to work with a new mixture of technologies: Classes were transmitted partially over phone lines and partially over a satellite system that was designed to help track Iraqi tanks during the Gulf War.

The sometimes tenuous video link required faculty members to develop more flexible curricula, and to allow students to work on alternative assignments in case the connection with their professors was broken. And the professors learned to be efficient lecturers—because of time limits on live communication with the ship—and because the sailors' free time was so limited. (McCollum April 17, 1998)

And the American search always is on for still newer ways to use distance learning. Another illustration:

. . . Helping prisoners to gain college educations before they are released would be a step toward preventing crime.

Technology offers a means to provide college courses to inmates and, as important, to guards, who often need education to obtain a promotion. Guards' odd work hours often make obtaining an education difficult. The education could be provided inside the prisons without any risk to professors or extra expense for security . . .

[An electronic] classroom could be set up in each prison for $20,000 . . . Prisoners . . . would see their professors on television and interact with them via computer or by voice . . .

In all likelihood, only a small percentage of prisoners would take advantage of the offer. But . . . [s]ociety would be better for it. (Editorial Page Editors, November 20, 1998)

As illustrated by the above examples, it can be difficult—or even impossible—to describe *"the"* American distance learner. While keeping the very wide range of this population in mind, this chapter's goal is to describe today's *most typical* distance student in the *most typical* American electronic learning settings. The relationship between distance learner characteristics, teaching approaches, and student services will be outlined.

Who Are Today's Distance Learners?

Dear Dr. X:

I am a [woman of color] 40 year old who has returned to school with a sincere desire [for further education in the helping professions]. My [own] history, as well as having been a single parent who was determined to break the cycle of poverty in my family, has deepened [my desire to] help others change their lives for the better.

At present, I'm completing my second semester as a [distance learning] student. So far, I have appreciated and enjoyed being a participant in the distance learning setting. However, there are times when the distance and inability to experience the teacher's actual classroom setting makes me feel that I will not excel. . . . I'm having difficulty feeling good about my progress in your class.

For the most part, I enjoy using the experiential activities in the course guide, but I'm having difficulty relating class lecture to reading assignments in the text. I'm not even sure how helpful, if at all, the reading material has been. I studied for [many] hours for the first exam, using your outline, and did terribly on the exam.

I am a serious student and am only used to getting A's & B's in my classes. I hope you will find ways to help us improve our grades, and the quality of your instruction. Please respond.

[Letter from a distance learner]

The common denominator among today's distance learners is that they look less like traditional college students and more often are midlife adults with families and everyday work-lives (Carl, 1991; Dille &

Mezack, 1991). Although today's distance learner typically is a nontraditional student, this may change. Since today's high-school students are so comfortable with the use of technology for information and for communicating, they may become increasingly open to new educational opportunities such as distance learning. Future distance learning populations may be more of a combination of different types of college students. As reflected in the above letter received by one of the authors, several characteristics influence today's non-traditional distance learners as they pursue higher education. These include: age, maturity, and development; cognitive-developmental factors; gender, ethnicity, and geography; motivations, goals, life choices, and demands; as well as previous learning, academic familiarity, and anxiety.

Age, Maturity, and Development

"*I am a forty-year old who has returned to school.*" Many main campus college classrooms today are filled partly with older, "non-traditionally aged", "reentry", or "returning" students. However, in distance education settings, they are the great majority—usually in their mid-20s to early 50s (Verdvin & Clark, 1991). For example, in one program, they were between the ages of 19 and 55, with the average being 31 years old (Schwitzer, 1997, November). They may be married, often have one or more children, and nearly all balance full-time work with attending school (Webster & Blair, 1998). They may choose distance learning partly to take advantage of its flexibility by scheduling college around their jobs, family responsibilities such as caring for children, a spouse, or aging parent, community commitments, and other interests.

These adult learners tend to have a greater sense of commitment and better understanding of the financial and time commitments required to pursue a college degree than traditional first-year students coming right out of high school (Webster & Blair, 1998). They usually have a more mature ability to act independently, are more self-directed, and take responsibility for class attendance, studying, and completing requirements (Schuemer, 1993). In turn, they generally are active in class (Schwitzer, 1997, July/August) and are active with advisors and student services (Ancis, 1997).

Adult learners also sometimes experience confusion about college rules, feel more entitled as consumers, and have mixed feelings about relating to faculty and administrators as authorities (Schwitzer, 1998). They seek expedient ways to pursue their degree requirements, expect more individualized considerations as "paying customers", and view instructors more as facilitators than experts and administrators more as resources than institutional authorities (Schwitzer, 1998; Webster & Blair, 1998). An illustration is the student who wrote the letter reprinted above; she felt comfortable candidly asking the professor to improve his instruction.

Cognitive Developmental Factors

"How should I relate class lecture to the readings?" Tied to age and maturity characteristics are cognitive developmental factors. Adult learners often are capable of more sophisticated (Oxford, 1990) and more self-directed (Baltes, Kleigl, & Dittmann-Kohli, 1988; Ehrman, 1990) learning strategies than are younger learners. These abilities are a good match with the demands of distance education formats.

Adult learners are developmentally different from traditional college students in the ways they typically interact with and understand information (King, 1990; Perry, 1970). Learners across the lifespan actively work to make sense of new experiences and new information by creating their own interpretations or explanations, and integrating the new material into what they already know and understand. As people gain more life experience and spend more lifetime interacting with their world, these individual interpretations and explanations, or "cognitive structures", evolve over time into progressively more advanced and complete ways of understanding. Cognitive advancement allows a person to think about more information at a time, consider discrepant and contradictory information, and understand a variety of perspectives on an issue.

As a result, traditionally-aged first-year college students often possess the dualistic perspective that there is a "right" and "wrong" answer to every issue and concept, with the professor, administrator, or parent being the authority who is the sole source of accurate information. This will be familiar to philosophy faculty who have attempted to move students from dualistic thinking to multiple perspective-taking in a sophomore ethics class, and first-year residence hall staff who have tried to move students from a strict "rules" perspective to a collaborative living approach. This does not describe typical distance learners. Instead, they usually are more advanced students who can adopt more relativistic positions, understand multiple student and writer viewpoints, take varying sides of an argument in class discussions, challenge the instructor, confront administrators, and reach their own conclusions.

Influences of Gender, Ethnicity, and Geography

"I am an African American female . . . as well as a single parent." The majority of today's distance learners—about two thirds in most studies—are female. In some programs, as many as 87% are women (Schwitzer, 1997, November). College enrollment is often sparked by a life event or transition such as job loss or changes, evolving career interests, new financial needs, or family changes. Women who are distance learners typically juggle competing responsibilities in their lives (Ancis, 1997). For example, because many maintain a large (or disproportionate) share of family responsibilities while pursuing their education, sometimes they must choose between work, class, and caring for an ill child on a given day.

Distance learning populations are culturally diverse. The economy, convenience, proximity and user-friendliness of distance education often make college more accessible to people who previously had considered it out-of-reach. About 20% of distance learners are African Americans, Hispanic Americans, Native Americans, Asian Americans, and others from non-White groups (Pugliese, 1994; Schwitzer, 1997, November).

Geography also defines distance learners. Key target populations for distance education are people who live in more rural locations and those who are limited in their ability to travel to the university campus for financial or life situational reasons. With exposure to interactive television, some people in rural areas discover new opportunities they had not previously considered or planned for through college-track academic preparation. Distance learning also reaches urban centers where, in the past, the cost of college education may have been prohibitive for some individuals. Many from rural areas and urban centers are first-generation college students who lack the advantage of financial or familial emotional support, or knowledge about adjustment to college demands.

Motivations, Goals, and Life Choices

"I have a desire for further professional education." Attitudes and motivations play an important role in satisfaction and persistence (Coggins, 1988), and adult learners tend to be highly motivated (Ehrman, 1990). Like main-campus students, some distance learners are motivated *intrinsically* by the desire for intellectual growth and the personal satisfaction of earning a college degree, while others are motivated by external, *instrumental* goals associated with job, career success, and greater pay (Ehrman, 1990; Schwitzer, 1997, November).

Most often, distance learners see educational attainment as a path to job advancement, professional certification, or a career change. Many already have work experience and significant real-life job responsibilities in their field of academic study. For example, when students in an interactive television program were asked about reasons for pursuing a bachelor's degree (Schwitzer, 1997, November), 60% said they were motivated by career considerations, including: to make a career move into a new profession; to be more qualified for a current position; and to qualify for a promotion or salary increase. One third were already working in their field of academic study—and half of those had more than 5 years' experience in the field.

When distance learners have professional advancement goals, they may be more involved, and more satisfied, with their academics (Wilkes & Burnham, 1991). They prefer learning experiences—class activities, homework, tests—that relate to their goals. In fact, their academic success and associated increase in motivation results in satisfaction with academic choices, resulting in even more motivation and effort (Ehrman, 1990; Strong, 1984). This, in turn, leads to further success and achievement.

Previous Learning, Academic Familiarity, and Anxiety

"There are times I feel I will not excel." While adult learners have the advantage of being more motivated than traditional college students, they have the disadvantage of feeling more anxious and less confident in the academic environment (Ehrman, 1990; Kahl & Cropley, 1986).

For many, academic anxiety is understandable. Some who return to distance education have not been in a classroom since high school. Some are returning to college after previously dropping out or discontinuing due to finances or other life complications. Others left school because of poor academic performance and are hoping distance learning will provide another chance to complete their degree. Until distance learning arrived, some never expected to be able to attend college at all, and so they did not engage in college-bound preparation in high school. Others may have some community college experiences on which to draw, but feel unsure about the "leap" to a "four-year school." Not knowing how to relate to faculty as authority figures can create extra pressure for autonomous adults (Steitz, 1985). Simultaneously, adult learners experience the compounding life pressures of work and family.

Anxiety and previous learning experiences both affect current learning. Athletes, public speakers, and anyone else who has felt the benefits of an "adrenaline rush" know that low and moderate amounts of anxiety (or "nervous energy") can help performance. However, too much anxiety can interfere with learning by hindering learner concentration and the ability to understand and apply new information (Ehrman, 1990; Steitz, 1985). High anxiety creates tensions that make working with instructors, classmates, and supportive staff more difficult. And it means the person usually must work harder than normal for less than expected results.

Being able to draw on past *successes* is an academic strength for certain distance learners. This would be an advantage for the business executive earning a lunch-hour MBA via telecommunications. But having a shakier background on which to draw can interfere with academic adjustment. For returning undergraduates and people new to college, old classroom skills, note-taking styles, approaches to assignments, and other academic behavior often are insufficient or wrong for today's needs—and particularly for the distance learning format, which requires a lot of individual student effort and learner self-reliance.

Distance Students' Learning Needs

In summary, typical distance learners are different from traditional college students. They are a diverse group of older students, often women, pursuing career advantages through distance education, are cognitively more advanced but possessing varied learning backgrounds, have multiple responsibilities, and expect academics to be relevant to their everyday lives.

An issue sometimes is raised as to whether being "a different sort of learner" *really means* being a less able, less satisfied, less successful learner. A recent commentary addressed this issue vis-a-vis gender, maturity, and motivation:

> Do women fare worse than men in distance-education programs? Some scholars claim that women and men behave and learn differently in classrooms, and that women are less likely to enjoy and to benefit from the remote setup . . .

> [T]wo studies of students in Indiana—one conducted at Ball State and the other at Indiana State University—found no . . . difference between male and female students in their satisfaction with distance-education courses.

> [Another study] found that gender was not related to students' anxiety about distance education. . . . neither was the students' age, marital status, or major . . .

> Nor does research on students' performance suggest that women do worse than men in distance education. A study of distance-learning students . . . at Old Dominion . . . revealed that the women had higher grade-point averages than the men did. Women earned a 3.16 G.P.A. in courses for juniors and seniors, whereas men had a 2.87 G.P.A. In graduate courses, the G.P.A. for women was 3.68; for men, it was 3.54.

> [Further] both male and female distance-learning students earned higher grades than did students in conventional versions of the same courses . . . [It appears] that the difference is because distance-learning students are, on average, more mature and more experienced than those who have just graduated from high school. The older students are probably also more motivated . . .

> The bottom line is that neither female nor male distance-learning students appear to learn less than students in traditional classes. In fact, the evidence indicates the opposite. (Koch, September 11, 1998)

Learner characteristics do, of course, have an impact on *how* we teach and support development at a distance. Distance learner characteristics require new *learner-centered* approaches that emphasize varied learning styles and recognize student variables such as developmental differences, previous learning, and gender and cultural factors, so that what is provided more closely matches student needs.

Meaningfulness

The first step to providing learning experiences that more closely match distance student needs is to enhance the meaningfulness of a) course structure and b) course content. Adult learners and returning students sometimes require more *structure* in order to understand the nature of a course's design (Ehrman, 1990). In particular, they are often less readily able to distinguish between major and minor assignments, between major course content and less central information, and the most important parts of lectures and readings from less important information.

In turn, they benefit from clear, detailed structure early on and throughout their academic program—in handbooks, in syllabi, in lectures and reading—that emphasizes key themes and makes distinctions between major and minor points (Cyrs & Smith, 1990; Cyrs, 1997a). Classroom instructors and advisors need to plan on frequent "question and answer" sessions to guide learners' approaches to their overall course of study and specific course material (Cyrs, 1997b). Aggressive advising is needed to keep students "on track" by helping them understand an academic program's structure of prerequisites and requirements—for example, to ensure they complete essential prerequisites before taking a more advanced course, even when this does not easily coincide with their work schedule (Ancis, 1997; Schwitzer, 1998).

Adult students also learn better when course *material* is relevant—and when teaching and learning methods enhance motivation. This requires varied, active teaching methods, shortening lecture presentations and increasing discussions and practical exercises. Real-life applications of conceptual and theoretical coursework should be included wherever possible (Egan & Gibb, 1997; McKeachie, 1986). Emphasizing actual case illustrations, especially from the instructor's own experiences, increases adult learner attention and adds credibility and value to class discussions. For example, psychology majors could design real working stress management programs and engineering students could solve real-life design problems.

Further, teaching and learning activities must be meaningfully related to learner cognitive-development. When a course includes more traditional college students with dualistic perspectives, they will assume the instructor (or advisor) has and will provide "the" answer (King, 1990; Perry, 1970). For example, dualistic learners may expect the instructor to map out "the" single best approach to a college math problem, when actually several routes exist. More dualistic students benefit from more step-wise instruction and from a supportive learning environment. They are best challenged by emphasizing relative points of view in class discussions and materials, and by experiential learning activities (Brown, 1998).

In contrast, older, more developmentally advanced distance learners who bring to class multiplistic perspectives and prior work experience will tend to regard the instructor as a credible, but not the only, authority. They prefer class discussions with opportunity for challenges and confrontations. Some returning students already are committed to a specific professional approach and may experience some discomfort or confusion when assimilating new learning. More relativistic learners benefit from greater diversity in course content, less step-wise instruction, and from challenges to make cognitive and philosophical commitments. Like dualistic learners, they also benefit from supportive learning environments and experiential learning activities (Brown, 1998).

Interpersonal Climate

The second step to providing learning experiences that more closely match distance student needs is to create an interpersonal environment that is conducive to adjustment, persistence, learning, and development. Distance students' interpersonal experiences include both their electronic classroom interactions with faculty and peers, and their interactions with student development professionals for advising, consultation, and other support services. As we have discussed, distance learning requires a high degree of learner self-directedness to complete an overall course of study and learner self-sufficiency to succeed at specific coursework. Still, students are more likely to persist when they experience higher levels of peer interaction and institutional support and are more likely to succeed at specific coursework when they have greater access to and interaction with the professor.

Even on-campus learners prefer and perform better when there is greater teacher support, more peer affiliation, and a supportive institutional climate. For example, students enrolled in learning skills courses prefer more supportive, interactive classes to those that emphasize self-paced learning (Scott & Robbins, 1985), career counseling clients prefer counselor-directed formats that include high levels of psychosocial support to self-directed career counseling formats without support (Robbins & Tucker, 1986), and "Freshman 101" orientation courses work better when they include a social support component such as faculty or peer mentoring (Schwitzer, McGovern, & Robbins, 1991). Such support becomes essential with the need to overcome distance education's geographic remoteness and the emphasis on technology.

More engaging teaching methods and more interactive classes also meet the cognitive development needs of adult learners. These methods include allowing for plenty of discussion time, holding debates, providing direct access to professors and administrators by telephone or email, and when appropriate, telephone or email access to classmates. One example is a televised group counseling course in which small groups were formed among students at different geographic locations using two-way microphone connections.

Further, while the traditional view of higher education stresses independence, contemporary learner-centered approaches are more multidimensional. Gilligan (1982) identified a pattern of predominance among men and women. Although this predominance is not gender-specific (or gender-determined), it is gender-related. Men tend to prefer individualized approaches to learning (and other life demands), while women tend to prefer learning (and addressing other life issues) in a relational, interactive, collaborative context. Combining opportunities for independence and interdependent learning will result in electronic teaching that is most responsive to different learning styles.

Looking beyond just preferences, both women and men are capable of both independent and interactive learning—and, in fact, both women and men appear to benefit most from instructional formats that integrate the two strategies. For example, combining two-way interactive classroom discussions over audio and video, or required computer conferencing and chatting, with self-paced learning formats to be used outside of "class time" is well-suited for distance learning.

Cultural Context

Responding to diverse cultures is the third step to providing learning experiences that more closely match distance student needs. On traditional campuses, growing numbers of students of color are enrolling in college (Ginter & Glauser, 1997; MacKay & Kuh, 1994) and most attend predominantly White institutions (Ginter & Glauser, 1997). However, retention rates have not increased in keeping with growing enrollments. For example, Steele (1992) reported that more than 66% of African Americans leave predominantly White colleges before graduation, compared with about 45% of White students. Learner-centered distance education approaches must include methods that address ethnic minority adjustment, retention, and learning needs.

One critical factor for students of color on the main campus is their experience of the social environment in interactions with faculty, peers, and student services (Allen, 1992; Ancis, Sedlacek, & Mohr, 1997; Hurtado, Carter, & Spuler, 1996). Adjusting to the institutional social environment is central to the success of students of color in mostly White settings. In fact, Watson and Kuh (1996) found that the quality of African American students' relationships with peers, faculty, and administrators tended to be almost as important as individual effort to their achievement.

Because faculty and peer interactivity and access to services is particularly important to distance students' academic success, student services must be accessible to the growing population of culturally diverse distance learners. Orientation, advising presentations, and other programming—whether in person, by telecommunications, through electronic media, or in print—should inclusively address diversity and social climate issues. In particular, orientation and advising will be more inclusive when specific topics are addressed, such as learner ambivalence about approaching or contacting faculty. Professional development for staff and faculty should include issues such as attending to the needs of students of color, social isolation, and student-professor relationships.

Distance faculty also must be aware of the cultural context of their instructional approach. For example, instructors sometimes use student competitions and individual achievements as learning tools. When these are applied to learners whose cultures do not subscribe to the value of competition, this approach is ineffective. Native American students targeted by rural televised instruction in South Dakota, for instance, tend to value community and collaboration over individual accomplishment and competition. In turn, this cultural position may be used to guide instructional methods which emphasize cooperative activities (Ancis, 1998). Similarly, since learning will be more effective when it is personally meaningful and relevant, lecture illustrations, case examples, discussion questions, reading assignments, and test items should inclusively represent the names, people, and situations important to students of multiple cultures (Ancis, 1998).

Distance Student Services Needs

Just as learner characteristics affect teaching approaches, they must be considered in the design of student affairs and student services for distance education. Who the learners are dictates how an institution's distance learning program is designed (Atman, 1988; Ehrman, 1990; Schwitzer, 1998). If a distance education program is intended to provide a complete, self-contained college alternative, it will need to meet the adjustment needs of a wide range of learners; if the goal is limited to supplementing conventional learning, limited services for a narrower population are required. Some programs are designed for the needs of many different kinds of students, while others have a very specific target group (like Navy personnel) in mind.

The role and amount of personal contact will vary from programs that provide substantial personal interaction with students (in person, by phone, or by computer) to those that provide little opportunity for personal contact with student services personnel. How to provide personal contact will depend on the program's technical arrangement and on learners' needs: Are they independently functioning, experienced college students pursuing graduate work, or wide-ranging learners whose previous college experience is limited to one or two community college courses? Learners with different learning styles need different sorts, and amounts, of guidance; some will prefer extensive guidance while others will not seek it out at all. People with more advantageous learning styles—for example, those with extroverted, intuitive, thinking, judging styles— should need less support than others (Atman, 1988; Ehrman, 1990). The bottom line is that the institution must help students acquire or increase skills and attitudes that are distance learning assets so they can maximize their ability to learn, develop, persist, and complete their goals in the distance learning format.

As four-year institutions expand into distance education, the student population will begin to be more similar to those who have historically enrolled in community colleges (Schwitzer, 1997, July/August). As with the typical distance learner, two-year college and community college students (Rooney, 1998, p. 1):

Are more diverse than ever before;
Hold full-time or part-time jobs;
Have families;
Have multiple obligations in their lives;
Have more complexities in their lives; and
Tend to enroll in school part-time versus full-time.

Therefore, community college student services provide good models for meeting distance students needs. The most comprehensive models include admissions, registrar, and orientation services; career counseling, advising, program planning, and goal-setting; supportive and developmental counseling services; and help with classroom needs, time management, childcare, and balancing multiple life demands.

Admissions, Registrar, and Orientation

All institutions must provide admissions and registration for prospective and enrolled students. One study found that three-quarters of distance learning programs also provide student orientation (Webster & Bair, 1998). In particular, administrators report that critical services included providing degree information, and specific orientation to distance education formats and required technologies.

Admissions, registration, record-keeping, and on-line financial aid may all be managed with use of technology. However, it is critical to provide: appropriate and efficient technology to facilitate asynchronous and synchronous communication between learners and student services personnel; website and email access; and easy student access to "help desks" or other technology support. Convenient access should be provided to on-line grade reports, on-line or telephone registration, and library resources. Electronic and print information, textbooks, and course materials all must be delivered efficiently, on time, and in a way that allows easy student acquisition. The student should also have access to a single contact person who provides prompt responses, ongoing feedback, and consumer service.

Orientation to college generally, distance learning, and technology should set the stage for a student's academic experience and create a learner-program fit that facilitates student success. In part, this will require student services to be more active in assessing student readiness for distance courses (Rooney, 1998). Van Wie (1998) discussed an academic advising model with two-year college undecided students that can be used to assess distance learner readiness and provide needed orientation services.

Fully prepared students need information about the everyday workings of their selected program and required technology. *Unready* students who are considering distance education but are not yet ready to make a commitment should be provided information about distance learning and how it will fit their needs and goals. *Unable* students who lack the academic, technology, life planning, or personal skills necessary for distance learning success can be provided more personalized orientation advising or counseling, skills training, or decision-making/life planning assistance. Finally, other prospective students who are interested in a distance program but are currently *unwilling* or *indecisive* about committing due to conflicting personal or life factors may need developmental counseling to solve their personal or interpersonal conflicts, or to improve their confidence and reduce their anxieties regarding a distance college education.

Advising, Career Counseling, and Program Planning

All institutions provide some form of academic advising, and one study found that two-thirds also provide career services for distance learners (Webster & Blair, 1998). Administrators frequently indicate that academic advising, counseling on course work, and career services are some of the most crucial services for distance learners (Webster & Blair, 1998). Academic advising and career counseling must be an active process that assists students throughout their distance education program.

Traditional advising focuses on the student's step-wise progress through an academic program, mainly addressing course of study, meeting requirements, helping the learner "stay on track," and handling registration tasks. Traditional career advising focuses on increasing student knowledge about: self (i.e., ones' interests, abilities, aspirations, values), the work world (i.e., different types of occupations, qualifications for job entry and advancement, work conditions and expectations, employment outlook), career-related educational choices (i.e., choice of program, degree, major, courses, to meet career goals), and decision-making (i.e., how to make effective career decisions that combine information about self, work world, and academics (Zunker, 1998).

In addition, more comprehensive student services appear critical to the retention and success of adult learners in distance settings who are less familiar with higher education institutions and lack exposure or experience regarding academic decision-making and need support to develop new life management skills (Dille & Mezack, 1991; Schwitzer, 1997, November; Webster & Blair, 1998). Although these services also are commonly offered to traditionally-aged main-campus students, they are essential for distance learners who must develop new skills to manage higher education demands. These comprehensive services (Turner, 1998, p. 14) are designed to:

1. Teach course scheduling skills and advise students about course/curriculum selection as a process.
2. Demonstrate the relationship between different degree programs, majors, and specific courses—and career decisions, placement, advancement, professional certification, or salary increases.
3. Support students in their exploration of educational alternatives and choices;
4. Promote student decision-making skills and process.
5. Increase students' awareness of additional personnel, electronic, or print resources.
6. Help students use their skills and knowledge in academic programs across available disciplines.
7. Provide interpersonal support.

Academic advising with adult learners thus must promote students' understanding about how specific components of an overall degree program are interrelated, the relative short-term versus longer-term benefits of certain course scheduling choices, the practical relevance of academic choices to career goals, and the meaningfulness of the educational process to real-life outcomes.

Often with this population, there is a need to address the ways educational, career, and personal dynamics combine to influence a learners' movement along their academic and career paths. Some of these learners may lean toward making *hasty decisions* about coursework and career moves that are unrealistic, or do not consider all options. Advisors and career counselors may need to confront learners' haste and attempt to explore their reasoning; other learners may *postpone* making educational choices (choosing a degree program) or taking action (finally enrolling in advanced statistics) (Van Wie, 1998). Effective advising with these people usually involves exploring the reasons for postponement while encouraging an action plan.

Some learners present the advising/career issue of *equipotentiality*; that is, they have the capabilities and opportunities to pursue a number of equally attractive, competing options. The advising/career development task in this case is to focus less on abilities and interests and more on factors, such as: acceptable levels of risk, shortest path to greatest gains, greatest flexibility to pursue alternative options later on, comparative financial rewards, and opportunities to pursue avocational interests. Other learners allow unproductive *perfectionism* to create inflexibility and indecisiveness due to "waiting it out" for the "perfect" option—perfect course schedule, educational arrangement, or school-to-career application. This requires helping the student explore his or her belief system (or attitudes) and decision-making process (Van Wie, 1998).

Two additional ways that educational and personal dynamics combine is when *fear of failure* or *consequences for significant others* influence choices and behavior. Those who fear failure to some degree—especially if prior learning experiences were not positive—may need to confront self-doubts through advising conversations and by "trying out" a course or two and incrementally adding to their load later. Those concerned about the effects of their educational pursuits on others may need to resolve how their academic commitments may change things at home (more limited time available for children or spouse) or at work (a promotion may mean different relationships with colleagues or new supervisory responsibilities). While these issues might sound more like personal counseling than advising and career counseling, they are likely to be part of the distance learner's advising dialogue. Often the advisor will be the student's primary institutional support at a distance. In turn, distance service providers must be open to crossing the traditional lines found between student affairs offices on conventional campuses (Van Wie, 1998).

Distance advising and career services can be provided through telephone tie-ins to main campus academic advisors and career counselors; toll-free phone lines, voice mail, and email; geographically remote on-site support and advising from site directors and additional student services personnel; access to local community college counselors; on-site teaching assistants; faculty advisors with "virtual" office hours; on-line systems that provide immediate feedback; videotaped advising/counseling segments; and on-line group advising chats. In addition, distance learners sometimes make periodic visits to an institution's main campus for services.

Psychological Counseling

Currently, psychological counseling services are not as available to distance learners as are admissions, advising, and career assistance. According to Webster and Blair (1998), less than one-third of distance programs provide counseling programs. However, institutional administrators tend to believe that counseling and motivational support are integral to distance learners' academic success.

Institutions provide access to psychological counseling in different ways. Some provide direct services via telephone or synchronous computer chatting, while asynchronous counseling interactions can be provided via email. For in-person assistance, some institutions provide on-site staff, others provide access to local community college counselors, while some require that students travel to the main campus for personal counseling. In many cases, student services staff serve a generalist function that combines "educational services" (admissions, registration, and academic counseling), testing and placement, career services (career counseling and placement), and personal counseling. For the generalist, the personal counseling function most often is in the form of mentoring and providing motivational support. Finally, student affairs staff are referral resources for assistance outside the university or college.

The most comprehensive psychological counseling programs offer three types of services: prevention, developmental intervention, and psychotherapeutic intervention (Drum & Lawler, 1988). Institutions must make local determinations about whether a particular service delivery mode is suitable, feasible, effective, and ethical for addressing specific concerns and for work with specific client populations. *Preventive* services are intended to prevent or forestall the onset of problems or personal-emotional needs. While the need for assistance may not currently exist, possible or probable susceptibility to a particular student problem is evident. On conventional campuses, examples include the possibility of social adjustment problems among first-year students, body-image eating-related concerns among young women, or alcohol-related difficulties. In comparison, distance learners may present stress management difficulties related to juggling school, work and family, and marital strain related to the life changes that college pursuits might spark.

The prevention methodology used most often by college counselors relies on provision of information to increase understanding, enhance attitudes, and promote healthier behavior (Drum & Lawler, 1988). Prevention methods include educational formats such as lectures, videotaped or media presentations, brochures, informative websites, and an emphasis on student self-assessment. Informative prevention methods are well-suited to distance education. They can be stand-alone programs or part of orientation and advising meetings; in-person or prerecorded; occur individually or in groups; and make use of electronic media or print. For example, distance student handbooks can include a section dealing with prevention. These passive methods are relatively inexpensive and have the potential to reach large audiences.

Developmental interventions are relevant when the need for assistance has already emerged or is clearly present. Developmental interventions facilitate normal adjustment and development by assisting people to add new skills or dimensions to their lives, or prevent a derailment of adjustment and development due to psychological dysfunction. For example, on conventional campuses, students may experience romantic relationship problems and identity confusion (Drum & Lawler, 1988). Distance learners may experience role confusion as they return to student status; confront competing life demands such as parenting, work, and study; face marital separation or divorce; or negotiate care-taking problems associated with children or elders.

Developmental counseling occurs when a problem exists, causes some difficulties, and has the potential to grow—but currently falls short of severely impairing the individual's daily adjustment. The goals of developmental counseling are to promote planful self-directed inquiry, and develop problem-solving strategies, without making the help-seeking experience seem too threatening (counselors refer to this as maintaining low levels of resistance).

Individual counseling for developmental concerns usually is brief, supportive, and problem-focused. The emphasis usually is on self-inquiry, generating solutions, and behavior change (Drum & Lawler, 1988). We believe developmental counseling requires face-to-face contact. However, sometimes it occurs via communication technology such as telephone and synchronous computer interactions. Support regarding developing counseling issues can be provided by student affairs generalists. However, counseling interventions for developmental concerns must be provided only by appropriate counseling professionals. When the counselor and student are face-to-face, developmental counseling can be provided individually, or in workshops and brief group formats that emphasize education about the counseling topic, cognitive interventions, self-monitoring, problem-solving, skill development, and coping strategies. Group arrangements efficiently utilize counselor resources. Our view is that individual and group counseling for developmental concerns should be facilitated in-person by on-site counselors or community college personnel. However, it is likely that a growing practice will be the use of two-way audio-video technology that brings counselor and students together through microphones and monitors, or electronically using computer chat rooms. Because the ethical, competent practice of student services may include only those practices for which there is conceptual and empirical support, research first will be needed to determine outcomes and other factors associated with developmental counseling formats using communications technology.

Psychotherapeutic approaches are utilized to address recurring life issues, clinical problems, and "entrenched dysfunctional life patterns" (Drum & Lawler, 1988, p.13). On conventional campuses and for distance learners, the most common difficulties include depression and anxiety disorders. In most situations, problems requiring psychotherapeutic approaches interfere with the learner's ability to adequately meet normal academic requirements. Psychotherapeutic approaches include more intensive individual and group psychotherapy. In some cases, psychological assessment and medical consultation are required to assist the clinician.

Student services generalists can be supportive of students who are experiencing more advanced difficulties, and faculty may accommodate their special needs where possible. However, psychotherapeutic services must be provided only by appropriately trained and licensed clinicians, such as psychologists, clinical social workers, and mental health counselors. Further, our view is that more intensive psychotherapy requires face-to-face contact and cannot be provided via long-distance technology. In turn, students in need of this service will require local mental health professionals who are on-site, available at local community colleges, or practicing in their communities. Students in rural locations and other under-served areas may have to travel to neighboring localities or the main campus, if possible, for psychotherapeutic services. Most often, counseling centers are limited to programs that directly support the institution's academic mission, so that distance learners usually must explore their own treatment options outside the institution when more extensive help is required.

Instrumental Support

Additional services for distance learners are those that facilitate the students' everyday handling of their distance education. These will vary greatly from program to program. Lunch-hour learners in corporate workplace receptor classrooms, students learning at home by computer or television, and those attending remote campuses can expect different types and levels of instrumental support needs.

The most common instrumental supports for typical distance learners are on-line educational programs: technical help, library access, writing assistance, math assistance, study skills, and tutoring (Rooney, 1998; Webster & Blair, 1998). Adequate library access, in particular, is commonly cited as a critical requirement. Also cited as critical are financial programs: telephone and on-line financial aid services, special tuition payment and deferment programs, employee assistance plans, and veteran affairs.

Some distance programs provide access to daycare, a particular convenience for adult learners balancing work, parenting, and school. Carpooling and group travel arrangements might also be needed. Adult learner needs for greater scheduling flexibility can be met by having space, personnel, and arrangements for learners to watch lecture videotapes or make-up exams and assignments (Ancis, 1997; Schwitzer, 1998). For example, one institution provides proctored exam make-up services every Saturday morning (Ancis, 1997). Cohorts who learn at home by computer or broadcast television may need an institutional space to periodically meet together. Even provisions such as food services (cafeteria or vending), book stores, lounge areas, limited student activities, and recreation should not be overlooked. In this case, institutions delivering distance learning may arrange cooperative agreements with community college sites, corporate business centers, public libraries, local college campuses, hotel/convention centers, or other local enterprises with the physical space, personnel, and other resources to offer meeting rooms, etc., to distance learners in their own communities.

Summary

Student affairs divisions are most effective when their services and practices closely match the needs of constituent learners. Today's distance learners are non-traditionally aged students who have multiplistic life-views and many already-formed attitudes and beliefs; are culturally, ethnically, and geographically diverse; have substantial personal and occupational life experiences; and, on one hand, are motivated by professional goals and opportunities for advancement or positive changes in life situation, but, on the other hand, may be challenged by previous learning experiences or limited academic familiarity. In turn, distance academic programs and distance student services must match these learners' specific needs. In order to promote distance students' college adjustment and development, distance services must use information and communication technologies to assist students with smooth admissions and registration; provide effective orientation, advising, and career counseling at a distance; support students experiencing psychological counseling needs; and provide instrumental help. In order to promote distance student learning, distance classes must emphasize the meaningfulness of course material, use learner-centered instructional approaches, provide positive interpersonal climates, and attend to diverse population issues. The remaining chapters more closely examine methods for meeting distance student needs by promoting adjustment, development, and learning.

References

Allen, W. R. (1992). The color of success: African-American college student outcomes at predominantly White and historically Black public colleges and universities. *Harvard Educational Review, 62,* 26-44.

Ancis, J. R., Sedlacek, W. E., & Mohr, J. J. (1998). *Student perceptions of the campus cultural climate by race* (Research Report No. 1-98). College Park, MD: University of Maryland, Counseling Center.

Ancis, J. R. (1997). *TELETECHNET assessment report: Human Services Counseling program*. Norfolk, VA: Old Dominion University, Department of Educational Leadership and Counseling.

Ancis, J. R. (1998). Cultural competency training at a distance: Challenges and strategies. *Journal of Counseling and Development, 76,* 134-143.

Atman, K. (1988). Psychological type elements and goal accomplishment style: Implications for distance education. *The American Journal of Distance Education, 2,* (3) 36-44.

Baltes, P. B., Kliegl, R., & Dittmann-Kohli, F. (1988). On the locus of training gains in research on the plasticity of fluid intelligence in old age. *Journal of Educational Psychology, 80,* (3) 392-400.

Brown, N. (1998). *Psychoeducational Groups*. Muncie, IN: Accelerated Development, Inc.

Carl, D. L. (1991, May). Electronic distance learning: Positives outweigh negatives. *T.H.E. Journal,* 67-70.

Coggins, C. C. (1988). Preferred learning styles and their impact on completion of external degree programs. *The American Journal of Distance Education, 2,* 25-37.

Cyrs, T. E. (Ed.). (1997a). *Teaching and learning at a distance: What it takes to effectively design, deliver, and evaluate programs*. San Francisco: Jossey-Bass.

Cyrs, T. E. (Ed.). (1997b). Competence in teaching at a distance. In T. E. Cyrs (Ed.). *Teaching and learning at a distance: What it takes to effectively design, deliver, and evaluate programs*. San Francisco: Jossey-Bass.

Cyrs, T. E., & Smith, F. A. (1990). *Teleclass teaching: A resource guide* (2nd ed.). Las Cruces: Center for Educational Development, New Mexico State University.

Dille, B., & Mezack, M. (1991). Identifying predictors of high risk among community college telecourse students. *The American Journal of Distance Education, 5,* 24-35.

Drum, D. J., & Lawler, A. C. (1988). *Developmental interventions: Theories, principles, and practice*. Columbus, OH: Merrill Publishing Co.

Editorial Page Editors. (November 20, 1998). College behind bars: Alternative to crime: Education could be provided inside prisons without any risk to professors or extra expense for security. *The Virginian-Pilot,* Norfolk, VA. p. B10.

Egan, M. W., & Gibb, G. S. (1997). Student-centered instruction for the design of telecourses. In T. E. Cyrs, (Ed.). *Teaching and learning at a distance: What it takes to effectively design, deliver, and evaluate programs*. San Francisco: Jossey-Bass.

Ehrman, M. (1990). Psychological factors and distance education. *The American Journal of Distance Education, 4,* (1) 10-24.

Gilligan, C. (1982). *In a different voice: Psychological theory and women's development*. Cambridge, MA: Harvard University Press.

Ginter, E. J., & Glauser, A. (1997). *Instructor's manual—The right start*. New York: Addison Wesley Longman.

Hewitt, R. L., Hart, J. K., Jefferson, D. L., & Thomas, C. R. (1990, November). *A developing model: Multi-level partnership as a tool for minority student retention*. Paper presented at the annual Black Student Retention in Higher Education Conference, Baltimore, MD.

Hurtado, S., Carter, D. F., & Spuler, A. (1996). Latino student transition to college: Assessing difficulties and factors in successful college adjustment. *Research in Higher Education, 37,* 135-157.

Kahl, T. N., & Cropley, A. J. (1986). Face-to-face versus distance learning: Psychological consequences and practical implications. *Distance Education, 7,* 38-48.

King, P. (1990). Assessing development from a cognitive-developmental perspective. In D. G. Creamer (Ed.)., *College student development: Theory and practice for the 1990s*. Alexandria, VA: American College Personnel Association.

Koch, J. V. (September 11, 1998). How women actually perform in distance education. *The Chronicle of Higher Education*.

Kuh, G., Schuh, J., Whitt, E., Andreas, A. E., Lyons, J. W., Strange, C. C., Krehbiel, L. E., & MacKay, K. A. (1991). *Involving colleges: Successful approaches to fostering student learning and development outside the classroom*. San Francisco: Jossey-Bass.

MacKay, K. A., & Kuh, G. D. (1994). A comparison of student effort and educational gains of Caucasian and African-American students at predominantly white colleges and universities. *Journal of College Student Development, 35,* 217-223.

McCollum, K. (April 17, 1998). All M.B.A.'s on deck! Old Dominion U. uses technology to teach business courses on an aircraft carrier. *Chronicle of Higher Education*, Information Technology Page.

McKeachie, W. J. (1986). *Teaching tips: A guidebook for the beginning college teacher*. (8th ed.). Lexington, MA: Heath.

Oxford, R. (1990). Styles, strategies, and aptitude: Important connections for language learners. In T. Parry & C. W. Stansfield (Eds.)., *Language aptitude: Past, present, and future research*. Englewood Cliffs, NJ: Prentice-Hall.

Peterson's Guides. (1993). *The electronic university: A guide to distance learning*. Princeton, NJ: Peterson's Guides.

Perry, W., Jr. (1970). *Intellectual and ethical development in the college years: A scheme*. New York: Holt, Rhinehart, & Winston.

Pugliese, R. R. (1994). Telecourse persistence and psychological variables. *The American Journal of Distance Education, 8,* (3) 22-39.

Robbins, S. B., & Tucker, K. (1986). Relation of goal instability to self-directed and interactional career counseling workshops. *Journal of Counseling Psychology, 33,* 418-424.

Rooney, M. (1998, March). *Technology, distance learning, student affairs: All in the same breath?* Paper presented at the annual meeting of the American College Student Personnel Association, St. Louis, MO.

Schuemer, R. (1993). *Some psychological aspects of distance education*. (ERIC Document Reproduction Service No. ED 357 266).

Schwitzer, A. M. (July/August, 1997). Supporting student learning from a distance. *About Campus, 2,* (3) 27-29.

Schwitzer, A. M. (1997, November). *Assessing climate, satisfaction, and learning among students in distance learning classrooms*. Paper presented at the State Council on Higher in Virginia Annual Conference on Student Assessment, Virginia Beach, VA.

Schwitzer, A. M. (1998, November). *Teaching at a distance*. Paper presented at the annual conference on teaching and technology of the Southeast Psychological Association, Harrisonburg, VA.

Schwitzer, A. M., Griffin, O. T., Ancis, J. R., & Thomas, C. R. (in press). Social adjustment experiences of African American college students. *Journal of Counseling and Development*.

Schwitzer, A. M., McGovern, T. V., & Robbins, S. B. (1991). Influences of goal instability and social support on college adjustment. *Journal of College Student Development, 34,* 21-25.

Schwitzer, A. M., & Thomas, C. (1997). Implementation, utilization, and outcomes of a college freshman peer mentor program. *Journal of the Freshman Year Experience and Students in Transition*.

Scott, K., & Robbins, S. B. (1985). Goal instability: Implications for academic performance among students in learning skills courses. *Journal of College Student Personnel, 23,* 378-383.

Steele, C. M. (1992). Race and schooling of Black Americans. *The Atlantic Monthly, 269,* (4), 68-78.

Strong, M. (1984). Interative motivation: Cause or result of successful language acquisition? *Language Learning, 34,* (3). 1-13.

Steitz, J. A. (1985). Issues of adult development within the academic environment. *Lifelong Learning, 8,* 15-17.

Thile, E. L., & Matt, G. E. (1995). The ethnic mentor undergraduate program: A brief description and preliminary findings. *Journal of Multicultural Counseling and Development, 23,* 116-126.

Turner, E. (Winter/Spring, 1998). Moving from undecided to decided: Advising students about educational and career choices. *Eleven Update: The Newsletter of ACPA Commission XI - Student Development in Two Year Colleges, 8,* (3) 10-11.

Van Wie, K. O. (Winter/Spring, 1998). Unready, unwilling, or unable? *Eleven Update: The Newsletter of ACPA Commission XI - Student Development in Two Year Colleges, 8,* (3) 10-11.

Verdvin, J. R., & Clark, T. A. (1991). *Distance education.* San Francisco: Jossey-Bass.

Watson, L. W., & Kuh, G. D. (1996). The influence of dominant race environments on student involvement, perceptions, and educational gains: A look at historically black and predominantly white liberal arts institutions. *Journal of College Student Development, 37,* 415-424.

Webster, C. E., & Blair, C. R. (1998, March). *Student services and programs in distance learning environments.* Paper presented at the annual meeting of the American College Personnel Association, St. Louis, MO.

Wilkes, C. W., & Burnham, B. R. (1991). Adult learner motivations and electronic distance education. *The American Journal of Distance Education, 5,* 42-50.

Zunker, V. G. (1998). *Career counseling: Applied concepts of life planning.* Pacific Grove, CA: Brooks-Cole.

Chapter 4

Student Development: Creating Community at a Distance

A t a recent American College Personnel Association meeting, someone asked: "Technology, distance learning, and student affairs—all in the same breath?" We present an even more dizzying challenge: "Technology, distance, and *creating a sense of community* all in one breath?" Given what we know about the importance of community support to learner experiences, student development professionals must answer "yes"with innovative services and programs that deliver campus community to those outside the main campus. But so far, the concept of community has not received much attention in the distance learning literature, and has not received much emphasis when institutions discuss distance delivery systems or when they make bottom-line decisions about distance programming. This chapter first explains the role of community support in the higher education experience and then presents approaches to building community into distance learning programs.

Drawing on Experience:
The Influence of Community Support

Outcomes of community-building and social support programs on conventional campuses over the past several decades clearly demonstrate that positive interpersonal experiences and social climates are critical aspects of the extant college experience. A supportive/positive interpersonal climate helps students in three specific ways: (a) by promoting better adjustment to the demands of college life, (b) by promoting learning, and (c) by promoting student development.

The College Transition

Traditionally-aged students and adult learners face multiple adjustment demands as they negotiate the transition to college pursuits. Traditionally-aged students pursuing either conventional or distance education are transitioning from the home and high-school environment to campus and college-level coursework; adult learners, the predominant student body in distance education, are transitioning from previous learning experiences and the demands of everyday adult life to the special requirements of higher education. In turn, the adjustment experience of traditionally-aged students involves independently managing the mature demands of adulthood, while the adjustment experience of non-traditionally-aged adult learners involves integrating the new demands of college into an already-existing lifestyle.

Considering the learner characteristics described in Chapter 3, the general college transition experience for today's distance learner comprises a new combination of challenges, such as (Kahl & Cropley, 1986; Schwitzer, 1997, November; Verdin & Clark, 1991):

- Combining college demands with existing life responsibilities at home, at work, in the community, or elsewhere
- Handling the practicalities of schedules, transportation, childcare or eldercare, and access to technology
- Becoming oriented to the student/learner role, in comparison with other adult roles
- Gaining an understanding of higher education institutions generally and distance learning programs specifically; as well as
- Becoming acquainted with, and mastering, necessary technologies (Burge & Howard, 1990; Overbaugh, 1994; Wolcott, 1995).

Four Areas of Adjustment

More specifically, learners usually face four specific sets of adjustment demands when they negotiate the general college transition: *(a) academic adjustment* to four-year college-level educational requirements;

(b) institutional adjustment, or commitment to age-appropriate college pursuits, academic goals, and career plans; *(c) personal-emotional adjustment,* or the ability to manage one's emotional and physical well-being over the "long haul" of college pursuits; and *(d) social adjustment* to faculty, peer, and other interpersonal relationships at the institution, as well as changing relationships with family, coworkers, and others outside of school (Baker, McNeil, & Siryk, 1985; Baker & Siryk, 1984). For today's distance learners, the specific demands of college adjustment are particularly complex and challenging.

First, *academic adjustment* at a distance comprises three parallel tasks (Gibson, 1996):

- Adjusting to the requirements of the discipline or content studied (experienced by all college students)
- Adjusting to the process of learning as an adult (experienced by adult learners in main campus and distance learning settings)
- Adjusting to learning at a geographic distance (experienced only by distance learners).

Second, *institutional adjustment* for distance learners comprises two primary tasks (Billings, 1988; Sweet, 1986):

- Learning to use, and adjusting to the quality of, the instructional materials and the learning arrangements; and
- Learning to use, and adjusting to the quality of, the instructional and other institutional supports that are provided.

Third, *social adjustment* at a distance comprises both:

- Interacting with remote-site peer groups (Biner, Summers, Dean, Bink, & Anderson, 1996; Biner, Welsh, Barone, Summers, & Dean, 1997; Gunawardena, 1995); and
- Interacting in computer-mediated learning environments (Gunawardena, 1994; Gunawardena & Zittle, 1997).

Fourth, the primary *personal-emotional adjustment* task for today's distance learners is the ability to juggle two sets of situational variables or life circumstances (Powell, Conway, & Ross, 1990):

- The requirements of family life and family supportiveness; and
- The requirements of employers/workplace and employer supportiveness.

Adjusting High Expectations

Typically, learners set high expectations for themselves and their institutions. At the beginning of their college pursuits (Baker, et al., 1985; Zuker & Logan, 1990) and at points along the way (Schwitzer, et al., 1993), students usually experience periods in which unrealistically high self-appraisals are not realized, or when reality does not match their expectations of the institution or higher education in general. As unrealistically high expectations dissolve, students find that old coping skills are no longer effective in the face of new, progressively greater challenges. On traditional campuses, this is most pronounced in the first year of study (Baker, et al., 1985; Robbins & Schwitzer, 1988). The result usually is a decline in adjustment—a "bad grade" (academic adjustment), wavering about choice of major or completing a degree (institutional adjustment), increased stress at home or work (personal adjustment), or difficulties with a professor (social adjustment). Successful learners are those who persevere through the ebb-and-flow of college adjustment experiences.

Correspondingly, unrealistically high expectations at the beginning of distance learning pursuits typically include (Gibson, 1996, p. 26):

- an "inflated" sense of one's ability to perform relative to the effort that will be required; and
- an "inflated" sense of one's commitment to learning at a distance.

Successful distance learners are those students who maintain a relatively stable "academic self-concept" when inflated expectations of self-as-learner dissolve and more realistic self-assessments emerge (Gibson, 1996, p. 25). Distance learners who successfully maintain stable academic self-concepts tend to (Gibson, 1996):

- understand the process of learning as an adult (e.g., recognizing they might have different rates of retaining information than they did in the past)

- recognize the hurdles of learning at a distance (e.g., recognizing that "this whole way of learning" (Gibson, 1996, p. 27) may be harder than expected)
- recognize personal competencies (e.g., starting with easier classes and building up to more demanding ones).

In turn, distance students' views of self-as-learner are enhanced or bolstered by (Gibson, 1996):

- their accumulation of academic successes, for example, first on placement tests and later by meeting course requirements
- recognizing their own ability to master course content
- recognizing positive feedback and positive evaluations from instructors
- believing that instructors recognize, understand, or are accommodating of their life situation (e.g., believing the instructor respects the student's competing demands as a working mother)
- clearly understanding formal course expectations.

Adjustment, Learning, and Development in College: The Role of Community Support

Although self-directedness and the ability to persevere are critical to successful adjustment (especially at a distance), community support helps to minimize adjustment declines when they occur, lessens their impact, speeds up the ability to readjust and get back on track, and helps students maximize their abilities and inner resources over the long-term (Schwitzer, McGovern, & Robbins, 1991; Schwitzer, Robbins, & McGovern, 1993). As a general rule, an emphasis on social climate also results in better learning and optimal student development. When given the choice, learners prefer interactive classes that emphasize faculty mentoring, peer discussions, and participant relatedness (Scott & Robbins, 1985). Similarly, they prefer student development programs that emphasize leader support and student interaction (Robbins & Tucker, 1986).

In fact, the major college student development literature strongly suggests that adjustment to college, and subsequent learning and development, are all directly associated with the student's involvement in the institution's community life (Astin, 1977; 1985; 1993; Milan & Berger, 1997; Pascarelli & Terenzini, 1991)—or more specifically, that "involvement with one's peers and with the faculty, both inside and outside the classroom, is itself positively related to learning and persistence" (Tinto, 1975; 1993, p. 71). Supportive experiences can occur in classrooms (Astin, 1985; Tinto, 1993), through learning activities such as tutoring or participating in research (Anaya, 1996), or through intentional student development programs such as first-year orientation that focuses on student persistence (Pascarelli, Terenzini, & Wolf, 1986) and academic success support groups (Halstead, 1998).

Greater sense of community in the classroom—in the form of both teacher support and peer affiliation—results in better grades, greater persistence, and more positive learning outcomes (Schwitzer, et al., 1993; Scott & Robbins, 1985). Greater sense of community in the form of student services interventions—such as support groups and counseling programs—results in greater retention (Schwitzer, Grogan, Kaddoura, & Ochoa, 1993). Improved career direction, engaging in healthier behaviors, improved sociability, and more self-direction all are associated with supportive programs. Greater sense of community from intentional programs such as peer mentoring and faculty mentoring yield adjustment, learning, and development benefits (Schwitzer & Thomas, 1998; Thile & Matt, 1995).

In sum, the most effective educational practices inside and outside the classroom may be those activities that enhance opportunities for student involvement (Astin, 1985) and help the student become integrated into the academic and social life of the institution (Tinto, 1993). Therefore, student development professionals and faculty can potentially enhance students' adjustment and subsequent learning by a) providing social support experiences in the classroom or academic setting (Schwitzer, et al., 1991; Scott & Robbins, 1985), b) increasingly the availability of psychosocial support resources in the natural institutional environment (Cohen, Mermelstein, Kamarck, & Hoberman, 1985; Schwitzer, et al., 1993), or c) providing opportunities for student participation in intentional supportive programs and interventions (Schwitzer et al., 1993; Schwitzer & Thomas, 1998).

Different Benefits for Different Individuals

Further, community-building has different benefits for different learners. In Chapter 2, we described Schwitzer and Lovell's (in press) findings regarding distance learners and their need for interactivity. In summary, Schwitzer and Lovell (in press) found that:

1. Self-sufficiency is a key requirement of all learners pursuing distance education, since they must function outside the supportive everyday environment of the institution's main campus.
2. Some distance learners also will require sources of support such as personalized contact with faculty, opportunities for affiliation with peers, and greater interaction with administrators and student services staff.
3. And further, highly self-sufficient distance learners *and* those in greater need of support *both* experience greater learning and development benefits when the distance education format allows for more faculty-student and student-student interaction.

Schwitzer and Lovell's (in press) findings reflect the *curvilinear* nature of community support effects on distance student learning and development. More specifically, the impact of community support on a student's adjustment, learning, or development is different depending on his or her level of self-sufficiency. The curvilinear nature of the effects of social support on traditional college student adjustment, learning and development is well-documented (Robbins & Patton, 1985; Robbins & Tucker, 1986; Schwitzer, et al., 1993; Scott & Robbins, 1985); Schwitzer and Lovell's (in press) study confirmed its relevance to learners in distance settings.

At one end of the "curve" are students with *lower* levels of self-sufficiency at a given time in their college pursuits. These students experience less self-direction; weaker commitment to their career plans, personal goals, or educational needs; and seem to have less ability to rely on their own strengths, skills, and inner resources to cope with life demands or carry on with ambitious plans. They may experience lower self-sufficiency as a general rule in their lives; on the other hand, even the most self-sufficient individuals experience periods in their lives—usually during times of high stress, significant challenges, or major transitions and changes—when they have lapses in their own self-directedness and self-reliance. For people experiencing low levels of self-sufficiency, community-building and social support serve a *buffer-*

ing or an *ameliorative* function. At this end of the curve, supportive interactions buffer individuals from momentary distress, bolster the person's sense of self, and promote their ability to effectively get going again. For learners experiencing low self-sufficiency, providing positive community support tends to prevent difficulties, produce greater retention, improve learning outcomes, and assist personal development.

At the other end of the "curve" are those students with *higher* levels of self-sufficiency. These students tend to be more self-directed; have stronger commitments to career plans, personal goals and values, and educational ideals; have stable ambitions related to work, academics, and other aspects of life; and are able to supply their own energy, motivation, strengths and skills, and inner resources for productive work. While they might be expected to have normal periodic lapses in self-sufficiency, they usually function, learn, and experience development in highly effective ways. Yet they, too, benefit from community. For people experiencing high levels of self-sufficiency, community-building and social support serve a *boosting* or an *enhancing* function. At this end of the curve, interpersonal interactions promote even fuller use of one's strengths, abilities, and a well-integrated sense of self. For the highly self-sufficient learner, positive community interactions tend to promote even more positive academic experiences, even greater learning outcomes, and even greater gains in personal development.

Finally, in the center of the "curve" are mid-road students experiencing moderate self-sufficiency. These are learners with adequate self-direction who are experiencing more-or-less consistent learning and development. They do not require the buffering effects of community support and do not fully take advantage of its potential enhancing effect. They benefit most from the ameliorative effects of community when, over the long haul, they experience occasional times of less self-direction, and when greater social interaction boosts their learning in specific instances in their academic pursuits.

Cultural Diversity and the Importance of Community-Building

Consideration to cultural diversity is integral to the successful development of community support in distance education programs as the student body becomes increasingly multicultural (Ancis, 1998). Students of color have several unique interpersonal experiences in predominantly White university systems. These include (Ancis, Sedlacek, & Mohr, in press; Schwitzer, Ancis, & Griffin, in press; Schwitzer, Griffin, Ancis, & Thomas, in press):

1. A sense of underrepresentedness
2. Direct perceptions of racism
3. The hurdle of approaching faculty
4. The effects of faculty familiarity

A *Sense of Underrepresentedness* concerns feelings of isolation, lack of support, and a sense that one is in the numeric minority. Students find the institution to be less friendly and warm than they had anticipated. Sometimes this is described as feeling "uncomfortable", "misunderstood", or "overlooked". A sense of underrepresentedness is captured by students who say they "always look for another Black person when you walk into the room" (Watson & Kuh, 1996, p. 417). By comparison, *Direct Perceptions of Racism* describes the experience of specific situations, statements, or actions perceived as racist. Beyond a general feeling of being isolated or alone, students of color often perceive the behavior of others in the institutional environment—peers, administrators, or faculty—as racist in nature.

The *Hurdle of Approaching Faculty* relates to a sense of hesitation, uncertainty, or difficulty when initiating interactions with faculty. Student initiative-taking in approaching faculty is perceived as both a necessary step in establishing working relationships with faculty, and an obstacle to be overcome. Sometimes approaching faculty is described as "kind of intimidating" or "too uncomfortable". This is captured by students who say "If I need help, I need help. Some professors will feel I need help because I'm Black"(Keong, Wagner, & Tata, 1995). At the same time, *Faculty Familiarity* tends to facilitate the process of initiating interactions. Students tend to be more confident about approaching faculty when (a) the pair is more demographically similar (when they are of the same race or gender); (b) their interests or area of study are similar or familiar (for example, English majors would prefer approaching English instructors); or (c) the student has had more extensive previous experience with the instructor and therefore has become more familiar with him or her.

Negative interpersonal experiences in predominantly White university settings can limit the ability of some ethnic/racial minority students to engage in learning, developmental programs, and other opportunities that are a part of academic life. For example, when students of color perceive faculty, academic supports, and developmental services to be uninviting and inaccessible (Stage & Hamrick, 1994), they must first deal with perceptions of underrepresentedness, racism, and faculty hurdles before tackling other academic demands.

Conversely, results of several studies suggest that when students of color experience warmer institutional climates—for example, those who enroll at institutions with actively involving and supportive environments (Kuh, Schuh, Whitt, Andreas, Lyons, Strange, Krehbiel, & MacKay, 1991; MacKay & Kuh, 1994)—they experience greater satisfaction with college and better adjustment, and are more likely to persist through graduation. Similarly, when students of color participate in programs that address existing community concerns by broadening students' access to a network of supportive relationships, enhanced adjustment and higher retention rates are found (Hewitt, Hart, Jefferson, & Thomas, 1990).

These concerns are especially important for multicultural populations in distance education. Because distance learning settings generally tend to engender initial experiences of apprehension, geographic isolation, and concern about establishing and maintaining academic relationships with faculty, peers, and the institution (Burge & Howard, 1990; Naidu, 1994; Wolcott, 1995), distance students of color, particularly, may experience the distance-learning apprehension typical of all students, in combination with heightened feelings of isolation, underrepresentedness, or disconnection often associated with being at a predominantly white institution. Because geography, technology, and time-lapses generally tend to be hurdles in distance learning interactions between instructor and students, among peers, and between students and institutional services (Ancis, 1998), distance learners of color may experience distance-learning disconnection typical of all students, in combination with heightened feelings associated with hurdles of initiating contacts with faculty.

In turn, less connectedness with the institution, less interaction in electronic classrooms or online courses, and less opportunity for familiarity with instructors and peers can limit the ability of some students of color to engage and persist in distance learning opportunities. Conversely, when instructors or student development professionals "humanize" the electronic classroom online course, or learning activity by actively, intentionally creating an accepting interpersonal classroom environment and attempting to create feelings of rapport, distance learning barriers such as feelings of underrepresentedness are reduced or broken down (Holmberg, 1985; Parker & Monson, 1980; Ancis, 1998). Similarly, using active learning methods that emphasize instructor-student and student-student interactions at a distance helps reduce feelings of disconnection, and, in turn, apprehensions such as those about racism, and increases student comfort levels (Simonson, 1995; Wolcott, 1994). Assessing students' affective experiences using internet interactions, writing assignments, and structured electronic classroom discussions also helps increase instructor-student interaction and reduce hurdles of approaching instructors from a geographic distance (Ancis, 1998).

At Risk Learners and Community Support

In general, a well-established sense of community, supportive institutional climate, and engaging academic atmosphere lessen these concerns and go a long way toward enabling those at-risk to seek out the supports they need. When students have positive interpersonal classroom experiences (Schwitzer, et al., 1991), positive experiences with student affairs professionals (Clary & Fristad, 1987; Schwitzer et al., 1993), and positive relationships with peers (Schwitzer & Thomas, 1998) and faculty (Thile & Matt, 1995), they are more likely to use supports when needed. Even when the outcome of institutional supports is only a modest improvement in grades, they very likely produce larger, more significant, long-term increase in retention and graduation rates. Overall, creating a sense of community in which learners feel they are part of the life of the university and have active, engaging relationships with other members of the college or university environment sets up the best conditions for at-risk learners to obtain assistance. As a result, they will be more likely to succeed academically and stay enrolled through program completion.

In particular, it is especially important for distance education programs to create positive, inviting climates because they tend to enroll more students with limited, mixed, or negative previous learning experiences who may be more academically at-risk. Most distance education programs advertise some sort of academic support service, such as online tutoring, library assistance, academic skill development, or telephone support.

However, research on conventional campuses shows that because most learners set high expectations for themselves and of their institutions, those in need of such services often do not seek out available academic or personal support programs (Friedlander, 1980; Walter & Smith, 1990). In fact, learners who seek out available resources often are higher-achieving students who experience relatively low risk of academic difficulty or developmental difficulty (Schwitzer, et al., 1991; Schwitzer & Thomas, 1998; Thile & Matt, 1995). Even those who eventually seek support tend to pursue assistance as a "last resort", once academic or adjustment difficulties are perceived to be a crisis.

A number of factors influence a person's decision to seek assistance. Although seeking support can help boost academic performance or adjustment to the institution, it can also threaten a help-seeker's sense of self-sufficiency or self-esteem (Fisher, Nadler, & Witcher-Alagna, 1983; Nadler & Mayseless, 1983). Put simply, help-seeking can appear contrary to cultural values centering around independence and the American orientation to *pulling oneself up by one's own bootstraps.* Conversely, for students from a collaborative orientation, there may be a stigma associated with seeking help from strangers, or outside of the family (or extended family) system (Keong, Wagner, & Tata, 1995; McGoldrick, Giordano, & Pearce, 1996). As a result, when deciding whether to utilize available resources, learners consider not only (a) the likely risks of avoiding assistance (e.g., continued academic decline) and (b) the potential benefits of seeking support (e.g., improved grades, coming off of academic probation)—but also (c) the social-psychological cost in the form of perceived threat to one's self-esteem or family honor associated with needing and seeking outside help (Gross & McMullen, 1983). When students have confidence in the student services offered, it is this third consideration that hinders appropriate help-seeking. Therefore, drawing on the extant help-seeking literature (Fisher, et al., 1983; Gross & McMullen, 1983), support programs at a distance are more likely to attract and benefit those students who are most in need when:

- students are provided information about the possible risks of avoiding assistance—and students have early opportunities for formal and informal self-assessment of distance-learning strengths, weaknesses, and needs—through electronic or online orientation materials, written information, and distance advising or other learner/ student services interactions

- students are provided information about the beneficial outcomes of distance services through (a) electronic, online, or written information reporting in understandable language assessment findings, university reports, and outcome studies regarding student involvement and use of the institution's distance services; and (b) teleconferences or online interactions with more advanced distance peer mentors who can provide real-life illustrations of the benefits and effectiveness of support-seeking

- marketing information, peer interactions, mentoring, and institutional requirements are used to normalize the use of support services as an integral, naturally-occurring component of distance learning pursuits—in order to reduce the social-psychological cost of helping-seeking in the distance learning environment.

Summary

Learner involvement (Astin, 1985) and interaction with the institution (Tinto, 1993) appear central to adjustment, learning, and development in higher education. Overall, professional experience and an extensive literature review indicate the central role of community-building, social climate, faculty support, peer affiliation, and support services in the adjustment, learning, personal development, retention, and success of learners—and the particular importance of community and social climate for non-traditional learners, students of color, and at-risk students. In the distance learning setting, a growing literature suggests that actively engaging learners in the distance educational experience is critical to reducing the effects of geographic distance, technological barriers, social isolation and loneliness, and heightened hurdles to involvement with faculty and student services that can come from learning while separated from the everyday life of the main campus. New methods are needed for creating community at a distance.

Drawing Up a New Experience:
Strategies for Community at a Distance

How do we create community at a distance? The selection of specific methods for community-building depends on the individual institution's distance learning delivery system and organizational make-up. Minimally, institutions that only deliver one-way distance education from the main campus (via electronic courses and online instruction, or broadcast classes) are limited to providing community and support through electronic media and telecommunications technology. Delivering courses using two-way interactive classrooms allows more opportunities, since learners can communicate and can interact with each other and with the instructor by video and other two-way technology, and they can use phone- and computer-lines to interact with one another from their homes or offices during class time.

When any of these arrangements is augmented by geographically distant field sites (such as regional academic centers, community college campus locations, or administrative field offices), there is increased opportunity for in-person contact and support (Stewart, 1975; 1987). Some institutions also provide distance adjuncts, teaching assistants, and field supervisors (at centrally located distance support centers) to supplement electronic and telecommunications delivery of classes. Obviously, this allows in-person faculty contacts and academic support. Other institutions take the lead in helping interested learners in different locations to organize periodic cohort support meetings, study sessions, and local get-togethers.

Other methods for increasing interpersonal opportunities include arranging periodic field-visits by main campus faculty and student services staff, or, traveling in the opposite direction, allowing or requiring distance learners to make periodic visits to the main campus for advising meetings, special class sessions, or intensive weekend courses.

Once the institutional constraints are understood, creative community solutions should combine the following elements:

1. Include distance learners in the life of the institution,
2. Establish opportunities for learner-faculty interactions at geographic distances, and involving faculty in student-centered community-building,

3. Establish opportunities for in-person and technology-assisted peer affiliation at geographic distances,
4. Provide group support services at geographic distances, and
5. Involve institutional leaders in student-centered community-building.

Including Distance Learners in the Life of the Institution

Institutions must view distance learning students as valuable and as important to the college or university as main campus students. It is essential to create an atmosphere that provides distance learners with the same resources, recognitions, status, and opportunities for participation as main campus learners in order to enhance their experience of community. For example, distance learners should be eligible for academic awards and other university honors. Where appropriate, registration materials, grade reports, and transcripts should be comparable to main campus materials. Clubs and organizations, especially professional organizations and academic major clubs, often are possible at geographically distant sites. Print or online newsletters and websites should be a part of any distance education program's infrastructure. Similarly, when an institution has a community newsletter or student newspaper, these should be provided to distance learners.

At one institution, Admissions, Alumni Affairs, Events Staff, and other services coordinate regional high school recruiting trips with visits to distance learning areas. In this example, an annual statewide bus tour that brings university officials and faculty to different parts of the state was developed into a similar opportunity for distance learners to meet personally with faculty and staff in a college night atmosphere that develops community spirit. These distance students, who attend two-way interactive classes, also receive site visits each semester from main campus administrators and staff who sit in on classes and express a personal interest in their needs. A televised graduation, complete with Pomp and Circumstance and on-screen photographs of each graduate, is also conducted by university officials.

Consumer Services

A sense of inclusion also is built by providing consumer-driven, user-friendly student services (either electronically or in-person at distance sites) that follow community college models by offering flexible evening and weekend hours and addressing the needs of nontraditional learners. Examples are career services that focus on midcareer transition issues and counseling programs that address family and marital concerns.

In particular, admissions and registration, academic advising, career services, and financial aid all lend themselves well to electronic delivery. Most institutions agree on these as essential distance student services and provide them in some form to distance learners. Adult learners are especially concerned that they use their time and financial resources wisely and so they demand comprehensive, accurate advisement. Distance learners should have access to a computer-assisted academic advising program that they can use at their convenience, which provides the following (Cully, Baum, & Miller, 1994, p. 40):

1. Detailed individual evaluation of all graduation requirements for each student.
2. Immediate access to information for students, faculty, and administrators.
3. Immediate assessment of progress toward graduation for students.
4. All requirements for graduation stated and tracked.
5. Requirements within the major categorized.
6. Approved degree program individually tailored, inserted, and tracked.
7. Number of classes, number of semester hours, and combinations of each tracked.
8. Prerequisites for required courses listed.
9. Narrative information provided.
10. All credit, substitutions, and waivers included.
11. Instant update capability.
12. Opportunity to "shop" for a major and immediately review change of major consequences.
13. Requirements tracked as frequently as every semester, but each student tracked by date of entry into major.
14. Two or more majors capable of being tracked.

Online career services should provide easy access to: interest inventories and other career guidance programs that help with career decision-making; information about resume design, interviewing skills, and preparing for mid-life job change or career advancement; job placement data such as position descriptions, employer databases, job vacancy listings; and job search tracking. Online financial aid services should provide access to financial aid program databases, student and program requirements and qualifications, financial self-assessments and eligibility checklists for student review, and samples of forms and materials for the major federal, state, private, and institutional aid packages.

In addition, adequate "bookstore" type supplies must be provided by mail or at satellite centers, and comprehensive library services should be available online or through interlibrary loan programs. Distance learners consistently report that receiving registration and course-related materials in a timely, dependable manner is key to their satisfaction. Further, distance learners emphasize a need for *non-contradictory* information when dealing with different institutional staff, services, or offices (Hardy & Boaz, 1997). Assigning students a primary telephone or email advisor, or having an electronic ombudsperson, can assist learners as they negotiate the institutional system from a distance, and can help ensure they receive reliable, non-contradictory information. Attending to these details not only benefits distance learners directly with well-aimed basic services, it also communicates the institution's commitment to the student's experience.

Faculty Support of Distance Learners

As seen in the previous chapter, distance education requires changing faculty roles. When faculty adopt more actively engaging teaching and learning methods, they become more closely connected with the distance student's educational experience. Whether it occurs through two-way audio-video conferences, telephone, email, or online chat, the faculty-student relationship inside and outside the electronic classroom takes on new importance in supporting learner success (Dillon & Walsh, 1992, p. 16):

> Faculty who teach at a distance do indeed alter their roles . . . a positive relationship exists between the use of [interaction] and student involvement, motivation, and performance. . . . Student involvement [is] the foundation of all distance teaching activities. The extent to which traditional faculty roles are modified by teaching at a distance

may be related to the type of technology used. . . . Although faculty need to understand how to use the technology, more important skills involve personalizing the instruction and incorporating student involvement into the . . . experience.

To support distance learners, faculty must add new mentor-like activities to their professor-student relationships. Specifically, new requirements of the distance student/faculty relationship include (MacKenzie, Christiensen, & Rigby, 1968):

- Diagnosing the students' readiness to learn
- Monitoring student progress toward objectives sought
- Recognizing and discovering a student's learning difficulties
- Stimulating and challenging students to further efforts
- Evaluating the quality of a student's learning in non-traditional ways, and
- Assigning conventional grades to work completed through unconventional learning methods.

By engaging in this type of distance mentoring relationship, faculty directly support students' academic performance, and contribute more generally to positive institutional community-building.

Further, faculty increasingly serve as an intermediary between students, technology, and available resources (Beaudoin, 1990). In addition to being skilled at curriculum content and the learning process, faculty must be able to help students utilize instructional technology as an educational resource. They must understand and help students understand how technological applications can create greater access to education by overcoming time and distance problems, and how technology (self-paced computer packages, videotapes, online resources, etc.) is responsive to diverse learning needs by delivering educational material in multiple formats.

Faculty Development

When faculty make the shift to learner-centered distance education, they sometimes express the need for professional development as they develop new teaching techniques, find ways to make information more meaningful to learners' everyday lives, and adopt new mentoring and student-support skills. In turn, student development professionals who are experts in learner-centered approaches and community-building will find new job opportunities available to them, such as: site administrators, distance program directors, program consultants and specialists assisting faculty who are retooling for distance education.

As an illustration, student affairs professionals designed the following basic "Teaching on Television" Workshop Series for faculty new to distance education. The training series addressed not only nuts-and-bolts concerns, but also student development issues. The technical topics addressed in the series were:

- Materials distribution and logistics.
- Syllabus, coursepak, and lesson plans.
- Effective visuals for television teaching.
- Library resources for distance learners.
- Copyright issues for television.
- Using e-mail, voice-mail, and online resources.

Beyond the basic "how-to's", distance student development topics for faculty included:

- Who is the distance learner?
- The adult learner.
- Active learning at a distance.
- Teaching strategies to promote interaction.
- Individualizing coursework.
- Creative assessment techniques.

As a result, distance education provided opportunities for faculty and student development professionals to collaborate as they designed and implemented programs that would support student adjustment, learning, and development.

Additional Faculty Support at Remote Sites

Further, for some academic majors or programs, faculty at a distance are not enough. Some courses of study require on site labs, field placement supervision, or tutorials. For example, natural science lecture courses taught through interactive classes, broadcast classes, or computer courses usually require on site lab work done in arrangement with local community colleges or satellite campuses. Here, on site lab instructors can offer in-person support that supplements the efforts of the main campus instructor. Similarly, local proctors sometimes are used to oversee test-taking; highly technical coursework, such as engineering and accounting, sometimes requires on site in-person tutors to augment classes and online instruction; and some technology, such as one-way and two-way interactive classes require local technical support. These positions all provide opportunities for local in-person support of distance learners.

Nursing, teacher education, counselor education, and other professional programs require capstone field placement courses—student nursing, student teaching, internships. Here, supervision and support for field work is provided by (a) local professionals in the training site/workplace with guidance at a distance from main campus faculty, (b) local professionals and local adjunct clinical faculty hired by the institution, or (c) local professionals under the supervision of mobile main campus faculty who make regular regional on-site visits. Licensing or certification requirements, professional standards, and local norms dictate the extent to which distance learners are provided on-site instructional support.

Peer Affiliation at a Distance

Community also must be built through efforts to establish supportive peer relationships among geographically distant learners. One concern about the distance education approach is that some learners will feel overly disconnected from other learners as they pursue their studies. Being part of an ongoing social group provides opportunities for buffering and enhancing performance through feedback, validation, and self-comparisons with others (Caplan, 1974). Peer support contributes to stable identity by allowing people to adopt relationship roles that contribute to a sense of shared life meaning, providing reflections of positive self-esteem, and offering encouragement.

Further, peer relationships are avenues for practical support. Peers can share information, facts, advice, feedback, etc., which might enhance a student's coping with academic and institutional demands (Thoits, 1986). They can also share tasks in order to better manage competing life responsibilities. For example, someone might take notes for another student one day when she is home with an ill child, or turn in financial aid paperwork for a peer as a convenience. In sum, peer relationships are opportunities for: dealing with emotional concerns, providing practical aid, sharing information about the environment, and sharing appraisals and self-evaluations (Cohen et al., 1985)—all in support of better learning and development experiences. The absence of adequate peer relationships is associated with anxiety, periods of despair, and a sense of isolation (Peplau & Perlman, 1982; Thoits, 1982).

Social networks may take the form of cohesive local cohorts. Students may be advised to take online or audio-video interactive classes together throughout a degree or certificate program. Study groups, support groups, counseling groups, and peer mentoring programs all help establish community relationships at distance sites. These can be regular or periodic in-person group meetings organized by faculty or staff, and led by participants themselves, college student personnel, or para-professionals or technology-assisted groups which use online, telephone, or audio-visual conferencing to meet regularly. Students can be encouraged or required to attend learning groups at the main campus on occasion.

Faculty in broadcast and two-way interactive classrooms can collect and show photographs of different students or different local sites, use maps to show where everyone is, and assign group projects across geography. Online classes can include brief biographies of class members or photographs where technology allows. Online discussion groups that are part of distance courses should require initial postings that allow students to introduce themselves to one another. Directories also can be developed which allow interested students to share phone numbers or email addresses and basic personal information.

Learners in online classes or other asynchronous courses formats can be linked together through on-line email peer mentoring programs. For example, Sanford, Zawacki, Kruck, Ahson, and Assanah (1997) paired first-year students in English composition and Introduction to Psychology courses with upper-level psychology majors. The first-year students in the program generally reported high comfort levels in the program; experienced positive, supportive relationships with their mentors; and received reliable institutional information from their electronic mentors—provided they remained linked to the same mentor for the duration of the program. Sanford, et al (1997) reported that when mentor assignments were changed during the program, mentees found the experience less supportive and the intervention was less effective.

Where technically possible, students should be allowed or required to work in groups and to complete group projects. When interactive classrooms are used, instructors often divide class members at each remote academic center into "small groups" for class activities (Ancis, 1998). It is also necessary to find a way to bring together students who are attending class from home, or who are taking class alone at a receptor classroom. In one program, students in interactive classrooms form "small groups" in class across an entire geographic region using advanced communications technology that allows them to talk together over the divide without disturbing (or being heard by) class members in other groups. When telecommunications technology is not available, online chatting and bulletin boards provide electronic methods of holding group activities. Outside of class, students can use the mail system, telephone, and fax to complete group reports and group projects.

Mentoring programs also work at a distance. Mentors, too, can communicate in person, by telephone, or use email and chat rooms. Pairing learners who are farther along in their distance education and have "mastered the system" with new students has the advantage of providing newcomers with a valuable informational resource and a source of social-emotional support.

On conventional campuses, mentoring programs have been especially useful for enhancing adjustment experiences of students of color in predominantly White institutional systems. For example, African American students are more likely to talk about academic and other adjustment concerns, follow through on advice, resolve difficulties, and develop effective strategies when they are involved in peer mentoring relationships (Schwitzer & Thomas, 1998). Similarly, mentoring is helpful for academically at-risk students when they act on suggested strategies for improving performance and when they follow through on mentors' suggested referrals to tutoring, academical skills programs, and career services.

Group Oriented Services

We have already discussed distance student services earlier in this chapter and in Chapter 2. Here we briefly make special mention of services that provide an opportunity for distance learners to meet together in small community support groups. This option is limited to institutions that utilize a network of local centers to deliver their distance learning programs—mainly when community college campuses, regional academic centers, and partner college facilities are used to receive interactive classes and video-conferencing, or to administer and support distance programs from the main campus. In these cases, program offerings similar to main campus services should be offered: counseling-oriented support groups; special population groups like women's groups and groups for African American, Hispanic, and Native American students; and academic support groups for at-risk learners. Based on local student demand, counseling theme groups can be offered to meet specialized needs, such as supportive groups for individuals caring for aging parents, parents of children with ADHD, grief and loss, or separation and divorce. Counseling groups have been demonstrated to be effective in providing the information and social-emotional support necessary for dealing with critical life concerns. They also are efficient, since they maximize the counseling and student development professional's use of time by bringing together several students for one meeting.

Involving Institutional Leaders

Distance learning bridges some of the gaps that in the past prevented many people from attending college. Just as on main campuses, one role of student affairs professionals is to educate institutional leaders, fiscal managers, academic program planners, and other administrators about the function of student affairs, student development, a climate of institutional support, and a sense of community in the academic lives of higher education's new distance participants. In fact, gaining the support of top institutional leadership is critical for implementing successful distance education programs and related student services (Moore, 1996).

However, administrators seem to have mixed views regarding the need to support distance learners. As institutions sort out learner needs in the new age of distance delivery, higher education officials express contradictory views about student services, such as (Webster & Blair, 1998, p. 5):

Students continue to need standard services to succeed.

Very different services are needed for distance learners.

Traditional services are irrelevant to distance learners.

> Distance learners should travel to the main campus to receive student affairs services.
>
> We need to develop better customer support and become more student-centered than ever before.

This sort of ambivalence may be due, in part, to the fact that very little research on distance student services has been conducted so far. As we discussed in Chapter 1, although student development professionals tend to emphasize a student-centered perspective of student services which focuses on the impact of student services on student adjustment, learning, and development, top administrators often adopt a contrasting or complementary management perspective, which focuses on allocating resources for academic programs and student services on the basis of long-range planning and measurable relationships between program or service implementation and academic outcomes such as enrollment, retention, and graduation (Kozloff, 1987; Schwitzer, 1997). As a result, student development professionals must take the lead in conducting local institutional assessment that determines the costs and benefits of providing various distance student services through different means and using different technologies—and in developing a solid research-driven literature supporting the role of student services for distance learner adjustment, learning, development, and academic success (Tolsma, 1997).

Institutions will continue to focus on learning outcomes (increasing knowledge, understanding, intellectual complexity) and the application of learning gains to life situations, practical skills, and career needs. National standards of practice for distance education currently are in development. For example, the Council for the Advancement of Standards in Higher Education (CAS) provides standards for student affairs practice on traditional campuses (Miller, 1997); parellel guidelines are in development for distance learning settings. National distance learning task-forces also are addressing standards of practice for distance academic degree programs (Albrecht & Jones, 1999). Following the guidelines set forth in the American College Personnel Association's (1994) position paper, *Student Learning Imperative: Implications for Student Affairs*, each student affairs division must develop a framework for distance student service delivery that complements the institution's distance learning mission, (1) "with enhancement of student learning and personal development being the primary goal" of new, creative, consumer driven services and programs, (2) which is integrated into a distance learning program's design and allocated resources "to encourage student learning and personal development," and (3) which generates a body of information about distance student development and bases its programs and practices on "research on student learning and institution-specific assessment data" (American College Personnel Association, 1994, p. 1).

Technology, Distance Learning, and Student Affairs: Pulling Together Changing Student Needs, Community-Building, and Student-Centered Learning

As described in Chapters 1 and 2, distance learning is bringing new alternatives for delivering higher education. As we discussed in Chapter 3, for their part, distance learners bring a new combination of learner characteristics to the college or university experience. We have emphasized in this chapter that technology and distance learning are not ends in themselves. They are means to bring new educational opportunities to a wider constituency. We believe that student affairs professionals are in the best position to be strong institutional advocates for a student-centered climate in the technology-driven world of distance learning. College student development professionals are needed to provide the services and community-building that assist learners to take advantage of the new technologies. Student development professionals must get in on the ground-level of their institution's distance learning plans and stay there! So far we have emphasized two critical roles for student affairs in distance learning:

- Using our background, experience, and professional training in the area of college student development to develop new responses to the new combination of needs and characteristics of today's distance learners at four-year institutions
- Using our background, experience, and knowledge-base in the area of institutional community-building and climate-setting to develop new methods for creating supportive climates and positive community relationships, and to offer effective student services using new technologies and geographic arrangements

Chapter 5 will emphasize a third role:

- Using our knowledge of, and experience with, student-centered instruction and active learning methods to help design effective academic programs for distance education and to be expert consultants for faculty and other institutional personnel who are changing their teaching approaches for distance education.

References

Albrecht, A. C., & Jones, D. G. (1999). *Association of Counselor Education and Supervision Distance Learning Task Force Final Report.* Stephenville, TX: ACES.

American College Personnel Association. (1994). *Student learning imperative: Implications for student affairs.* Washington, DC: Author.

Anaya, G. (1996). College experiences and student learning: The influence of active learning, college environments and cocurricular activities. *Journal of College Student Development, 37,* 611-622.

Ancis, J. P. (1998). Cultural competency training at a distance: Challenges and strategies. *Journal of Counseling and Development, 76,* 134-143.

Ancis, J. R., Sedlacek, W. E., & Mohr, J. J. (in press). Student perceptions of the campus cultural climate by race. *Journal of Counseling and Development.*

Astin, A. W. (1977). *Four critical years.* San Francisco: Jossey-Bass.

Astin, A. W. (1985). *Achieving educational excellence.* San Francisco: Jossey-Bass.

Astin, A. W. (1993). *What matters in college: Four critical years revisited.* San Francisco: Jossey-Bass.

Baker, R. W., McNeil, O., & Siryk, B. (1985). Expectations and reality in freshman adjustment to college. *Journal of Counseling Psychology, 32,* 94-103.

Baker, R. W., & Siryk, B. (1984). Measuring adjustment to college. *Journal of Counseling Psychology, 31,* 179-189.

Beaudoin, M. (1990). The instructor's changing role in distance education. *The American Journal of Distance Education, 4,* (2) 21-29.

Billings, D. M. (1988). A conceptual model of correspondence course completion. *The American Journal of Distance Education, 2,* 25-46.

Biner, P. M., Summers, M., Dean, R. S., Bink, M. L., Anderson, J. L., & Gelder, B. C. (1996). Student satisfaction with interactive telecourses as a function of demographic variables and prior telecourse experience. *Distance Education, 17,* 33-43.

Biner, P. M., Welsh, K. D., Barone, N. M., Summers, M., & Dean, R. S. (1997). The impact of remote-site group size on student satisfaction and relative performance in interactive telecourses. *The American Journal of Distance Education, 11,* (1), 23-33.

Burge, E., & Howard, J. L. (1990). Audio-conferencing in graduate education: A case study. *The American Journal of Distance Education, 4,* (2) 3-13.

Caplan, G. (1974). *Support systems and community mental health: Lectures on concept development.* New York: Behavioral Publications.

Clary, G. E., & Fristad, M. A. (1987). Predictors of psychological help-seeking on a college campus. *Journal of College Student Development, 28,* 180-181.

Cohen, S., Mermelstein, R., Kamarck, T., & Hoberman, H. M. (1985). Measuring the functional components of social support. In I. Sarason & B. Sarason (Eds.). *Social support: Theory, research and application* (pp. 73-94). Dordrecht, Netherlands: Martraus Nighriff.

Cully, B., Baum, S., & Miller, J. (1994). Academic advising programs. In J. L. Baier & T. S. Strong (eds.)., *Technology in student affairs: Issues, applications, and trends* (pp. 40). Washington, DC: American College Personnel Association.

Dillon, C. L., & Walsh, S. M. (1992). Faculty: The neglected resource in distance education. *The American Journal of Distance Education, 6,* (3) 5-21.

Fisher, J. D., Nadler, A., & Whitcher-Alagna, (1983). Four conceptualizations of reaction to aid. In F. D. Fischer, A. Nadler, & B. M. DePaul (eds.), *New directions in helping, Volume 2: Help-seeking.* New York: Academic Press.

Friedlander, J. (1980). Are college support programs reaching high-risk students? *Journal of College Student Personnel, 21,* 223-228.

Gibson, C. C. (1996). Toward an understanding of academic self-concept in distance education. *The American Journal of Distance Education, 10,* (1) 23-36.

Gross, A. E., & McMullen, P. A. (1983). Models of the help-seeking process. In F. D. Fisher, A. Naples, & B. M. DePaul (Eds.). *New directions in helping, Volume 2: Help-seeking*. New York: Academic Press.

Gunawardena, C. N. (1994). Social presence theory and implications for interaction and communication in the telecommunications-based distance education. In *Proceedings of the Distance Learning Conference*, College Station, TX, pp. 119-127.

Gunawardena, C. N. (1995). Social presence theory and implications for interaction and collaborative learning in computer conferences. *International Journal of Educational Telecommunications, 1*, 147-166.

Gunawardena, C. N., & Zittle, F. J. (1997). Social presence as a predictor of satisfaction within a computer-mediated conferencing environment. *The American Journal of Distance Education, 11*, 8-26.

Halstead, R. (1998). Academic success support groups. *Journal of College Student Development, 39*, 507-508.

Hardy, D. W., & Boaz, M. H. (1997). Learner development: Beyond the technology. In Cyrs, T. E. (Ed.). *Technology and learning at a distance: What it takes to effectively design, deliver, and evaluate programs*. San Francisco: Jossey-Bass.

Hewitt, R. L., Hart, J. K., Jefferson, D. L., & Thomas, C. R. (1990, November). *A developing model: Multi-level partnership as a tool for minority student retention*. Paper presented at the annual Black Student Retention in Higher Education Conference, Baltimore, MD.

Holmberg, B. (1985). *The feasibility of a theory of teaching for distance education and a proposed theory* (Report No. 60). Hagen, Germany. Zentrales Institut fur fernstudienforschung. (ERIC Document Reproduction Service No. ED290013).

Kahl, T. N., & Cropley, A. J. (1986). Face-to-face versus distance learning: Psychological consequences and practical implications. *Distance Education, 7*, 38-48.

Kozloff, J. (1987). A student-centered approach to accountability and assessment. *Journal of College Student Personnel, 28*, 419-424.

Kuh, G. D., Schuh, J. H., Whitt, E. J., Andreas, R. E., Lyons, J. W., Strange, C. C., Krehbiel, L. E., & MacKay, K. A. (1991). *Involving colleges: Successful approaches to fostering student learning and development outside the classroom*. San Francisco: Jossey-Bass.

Keong, F. T., Wagner, N. S., & Tata, S. P. (1995). Racial and ethnic variations in help-seeking attitudes. In J. G. Pinerotto, J. M. Casas, L. A. Suzuki, & C. M. Alexander (Eds.), *Handbook of multicultural counseling* (pp. 415-438). Thousand Oaks, CA: Sage.

MacKay, K. A., & Kuh, G. D. (1994). A comparison of student effort and educational gains of Caucasian and African-American students at predominantly white colleges and universities. *Journal of College Student Development, 35,* 217-223.

MacKenzie, O., Christensen, E. L., & Rigby, P. H. (1968). *Correspondence education in the United States.* NY: McGraw Hill.

McGoldrick, M., Giordono, J., & Pearce, J. K. (1996). *Ethnicity and family therapy* (2nd ed.). NY: Guilford Press.

Milan, J. F., & Berger, J. B. (1997). A modified model of college student persistence: Exploring the relationship between Astin's theory of involvement and Tinto's theory of student departure. *Journal of College Student Development, 38,* 387-399.

Miller, T. K. (Ed.). (1997). *The book of professional standards for higher education.* Washington, DC: Council for the Advancement of Standards in Higher Education.

Moore, M. G. (1996). Editorial: Tips for the manager setting up a distance education program. *The American Journal of Distance Education, 10,* 1-5.

Nadler, A., & Mayseless, O. (1983). Recipient self-esteem and reactions to help. In F. D. Fisher, A. Nadler, & B. M. DePaul (Eds.), *New directions in helping, Volume 1: Recipient reactions to aid* (pp. 167-188). NY: Academic Press.

Naidu, S. (1994). Applying learning and instructional strategies in open and distance learning. *Distance Education, 4,* 23-41.

Overbaugh, R. C. (1994). Research-based guidelines for computer-based instruction development. *Journal of Research on Computing in Education, 27,* (1) 29-47.

Parker, L., & Monson, M. (1980). *Teletechniques: An instructional model for interactive teleconferencing.* (The Directional Design Library, 38). Englewood Cliffs, NJ: Educational Technology.

Pascarelli, E. T., & Terenzini, P. T. (1991). *How college effects students.* San Francisco: Jossey-Bass.

Pascarelli, E. T., Terenzini, P. T., & Wolfle, L. M. (1986). Orientations to college and freshman year persistence/withdrawal decisions. *Journal of Higher Education, 57,* 156-175.

Powell, R. C., Conway, C., & Ross, L. (1990). Effects of student predisposing characteristics on student success. *Journal of Distance Education, 5,* 5-19.

Peplau, L. A., Perlman, D. (1982). Perspectives on loneliness. In L. A. Peplau & D. Perlman (Eds.). *Loneliness: A sourcebook of current theory, research, and therapy* (1-20). New York: Wiley & Sons.

Robbins, S. B., & Patton, M. (1985). Self-psychology and career development: Construction of the superiority and goal instability scales. *Journal of Counseling Psychology, 32,* 221-231.

Robbins, S. B., & Schwitzer, A. M. (1988). A validity study of the Superiority and Goal Instability scales as predictors of women's adjustment to college life. *Measurement and Evaluation in Counseling and Development, 21,* 117-123.

Robbins, S. B., & Tucker, K. (1986). Relation of goal instability to self-directed and interactional career counseling workshops. *Journal of College Student Development, 29,* 228-232.

Sanford, J., Zawacki, T. M., Kruck, M., Ahson, N., & Assanah, G. (1997, November). *Linking learners on-line: Assessing an e-mail mentoring program.* Paper presented at the annual Conference on Student Assessment of the Virginia Assessment Group, Virginia Beach, VA.

Schwitzer, A. M. (1997). Utilization-focused evaluation: Proposing a useful method of program evaluation for college counselors and student development professionals. *Measurement and Evaluation in Counseling and Development, 30,* 50-61.

Schwitzer, A. M. (1997, November). *Assessing climate, satisfaction, and learning among students in distance learning classrooms.* Paper presented at the State Council on Higher Education in Virginia Annual Conference on Student Assessment, Virginia Beach, VA.

Schwitzer, A. M., Ancis, J. R., & Griffin, O. T. (in press). Comparing African American and White college student social adjustment experiences. *Journal of the Freshman Year Experience and Students in Transition.*

Schwitzer, A. M., Griffin, O. T., Ancis, J. R., & Thomas, C. R. (in press). Social adjustment experiences of African American college students. *Journal of Counseling and Development.*

Schwitzer, A. M., Grogan, K., Kaddoura, K., & Ochoa, L. (1993). Effects of brief mandatory counseling on help-seeking and academic success among at-risk college students. *Journal of College Student Development, 34,* 401-405.

Schwitzer, A. M., & Lovell, C. (In press). Effects of goal instability, peer affiliation, and teacher support on distance learners. *Journal of College Student Development.*

Schwitzer, A. M., McGovern, T. V., & Robbins, S. B. (1991). Adjustment outcomes of a freshman seminar: A utilization-focused approach. *Journal of College Student Development, 32,* 484-490.

Schwitzer, A. M., Robbins, S. B., & McGovern, T. V. (1993). Influences of goal instability and social support on college adjustment. *Journal of College Student Development, 34,* 21-25.

Schwitzer, A. M., & Thomas, C. (1998). Implementation, utilization, and outcomes of a minority freshman peer mentor program at a predominantly White university. *Journal of the Freshman Year Experience & Students in Transition, 10,* 31-50

.Scott, K., & Robbins, S. B. (1985). Goal instability: Implications for academic performance among students in learning skills courses. *Journal of College Student Personnel, 23,* 378 383.

Simonson, M. (1995). Instructional technology and attitude change. In G. J. Anglin (Ed.), *Instructional technology: Past, present, and future* (pp. 365-373). Englewood, CO: Libraries Unlimited.

Stage, F. K., & Hamrick, F. A. (1994). Diversity issues: Fostering campuswide development of multiculturalism. *Journal of College Student Development, 35,* 331-336.

Stewart, D. (1975). *The roles of the part time staff in the Open University.* Milton Keynes: The Open University.

Stewart, D. (1987). Staff development needs in education. In P. Smith & M. Kelly (Eds.). *Distance education and the mainstream: Convergence in education.* NY: Croom Helm.

Sweet, R. (1986). Student dropout in distance education: An application of Tinto's model. *Distance Education, 7,* 201-213.

Thile, E. L., & Matt, G. E. (1995). The ethnic mentor undergraduate program: A brief description and preliminary findings. *Journal of Multicultural Counseling and Development, 23,* 116-126.

Thoits, P. A. (1986). Conceptual, methodological and theoretical problems in studying social support as a buffer against life stress. *Journal of Health and Social Behavior, 23,* 145-159.

Tinto, V. (1975). Dropout from higher education: A theoretical synthesis of recent research. *Review of Educational Research, 45,* 89 125.

Tinto, V. (1993). *Leaving college: Rethinking the causes and cures of student attrition.* (2nd ed.) Chicago: University of Chicago Press.

Tolsma, R. S. (1997). Managing information resources and services in a distance environment. In T. E. Cyrs (Ed.). *Teaching and learning at a distance: What it takes to effectively design, deliver, and evaluate programs*. San Francisco: Jossey-Bass.

Verdvin, J. R., & Clark, T. A. (1991). *Distance education*. San Francisco: Jossey-Bass.

Walter, T. L, & Smith, J. (April, 1990). *Self-assessment and academic support: Do students know they need help?* Paper presented at the annual Freshman Year Experience Conference, Austin, TX.

Watson, L. W., & Kuh, G. D. (1996). The influence of dominant race environments on student involvement, perceptions, and educational gains: A look at historically black and predominantly white liberal arts institutions. *Journal of College Student Development, 37,* 415-424.

Webster, C. E., & Blair, C. R. (1998, March). *Student services and programs in distance learning environments*. Paper presented at the annual meeting of the American College Personnel Association, St. Louis, MO.

Wolcott, L. L. (1994). The distance teacher as reflective practitioner. *Educational Technology*. January-Februrary, 39-43.

Zucker, R. F., & Logan, S. G. (1990, April). *The unkind, ungentle freshman year: Identifying and reducing stress in first-year students*. Paper presented at the National Conference on the Freshman Year Experience, Austin, TX.

Chapter 5

Student Learning: Student Affairs Professionals as Distance Educators

> There has always been a beguiling temptation to assume that all the problems of teaching at a distance can be resolved by the production of a perfect package of self-instructional materials (Smith & Kelly, 1987, p. 159).

> [The reality is] the potential reach and instructional impact of educational telecommunications systems [depends on measures that value] new relationships with learners (Duning, Kekerix, & Zaborowski, 1993, p. 187).

Student Affairs Professionals as Distance Educators

Student affairs professionals have taken the traditional lead in learner-centered approaches to higher education. Traditionally, student affairs professionals have had the major responsibilities on American college and university campuses for: designing, implementing, and assessing educational approaches that take into account the student's developmental experience, academic needs and learning styles (Creamer et al., 1990; Knefelkamp, Widick, & Parker, 1978); adjusting and readjusting educational methods to respond to the characteristics and needs of changing student populations (Fried & Associates, 1995); and emphasizing active, responsive instructional methods (Astin, 1985; 1993; Pascarelli & Terenzini, 1991) to produce the best possible learning outcomes (American College Personnel Association, 1994). However, on traditional campuses, student affairs professionals mainly have employed the student-centered emphasis, student development knowledge-base, and active learning methodology to promote learning "outside the classroom" (Pascarelli & Terenzini, 1991, p. 24)—for example, through support services such as advising, career services, and counseling, and when facilitating student programming such as orientation, wellness and prevention workshops, and psychoeducational groups. Sometimes they also provide some consultation to institutional leaders, academic departments, or individual faculty about student adjustment or student learning issues. By comparison, distance learning is likely to greatly increase the involvement of student affairs professionals in the academic life of their institutions because student affairs professionals will be needed in a greater capacity as experts who can design and build the "new relationships with learners" (Duning, Kekerix, & Zaborowski, 1993, p. 187) that will be required to produce distance learning outcomes in electronic classrooms.

Instruction through distance learning comprises three elements (Stewart, 1987): two-way communication, individualized instructional assistance, and student support services. First, there is two-way communication across distance between instructor and student. This two-way instruction takes the form of written communication, electronic communication, and telecommunications. Some communication is synchronous, such as in two-way electronic classrooms, while other two-way interactions, such as written and electronic communications, take place across discreet, asynchronous exchanges. Two basic sets of faculty skills are required for the two-way instructional communication of distance learning: (a) new course *preparation* skills and (b) new course *presentation* skills (Stewart, 1987). Student development professionals who are experts at active learning and learner-centered instruction will be needed as consultants and professional development providers for faculty in both the area of course design-and-preparation and the area of course presentation (or delivery).

Second, there is individualized academic assistance (Stewart, 1987). This includes remedial instruction (in-person at distance sites or across distance via telecommunications technology) such as teaching learning skills, technology skills, or basic academic competencies to prepare students for advanced college coursework; tutoring and study sessions to augment distance classroom or online learning experiences; and supervision of field-based instruction at distance locations. Increasingly, student affairs professionals working as distance learning generalists will provide more individualized academic assistance. They also will have a greater role as mediator, or liaison, between students and the instructor—clarifying requirements and course components and helping students and instructors understand the impact of learning exchanges, etc. Added to this list are new responsibilities as consultants and team-members when institutions and academic departments translate main-campus academic degree programs into distance learning offerings, or when new degree programs are created for distance learning (Stewart, 1987).

The third element, student support services (Stewart, 1987), was described in Chapters 3 and 4. Increasingly, student development professionals will be student services generalists responsible for providing a large variety of distance support services.

Based on these elements, student affairs professionals will have the following new or expanded roles in the academic life of distance learning: faculty development provider, academic liaison, program designer, and outcome evaluator.

Faculty Development Provider

> The emergence of increasingly student-centered learning activities . . . facilitated by new instructional technology . . . is contributing to a dramatic evolution in faculty roles, and raises fundamental questions within the professorate about how it will contribute to the teaching-learning process . . . (Beaudoin, 1990, p. 21)

Distance faculty require several specific skills they may not have needed, emphasized, or integrated into their main campus teaching repertoire. These include: techniques to increase student comfort with technology; techniques to humanize the electronic classroom; and learner-centered, active learning techniques.

Skills for Increasing Student Comfort with Technology

The distance learning classroom may be a new and potentially uncomfortable experience initially for both distance faculty and learners. For example, students often express discomfort and apprehension regarding communicating via telecommunications technology (Burge & Howard, 1990; Wolcott, 1995) This is an important issue because learner anxiety about new technology can interfere with feelings of connected-ness in the classroom and can interfere with students' abilities to learn at a distance (Overbaugh, 1994). Therefore, instructors should be equipped with classroom skills and exercises to increase student comfort with tech-nology. For example, learners can be asked to introduce themselves using microphone and video-camera in two-way classrooms, or through introductory postings in online discussion courses. Instructors also should be able to "normalize" the experience for students and to model effec-tive, comfortable use of technology. The instructor's comfort level with the technology used and with nontraditional learning formats will influ-ence classroom climate and learner comfort. Therefore, one professional development goal is to increase faculty comfort and expertise with dis-tance learning technology. Student affairs generalists will be expected to understand the use of technology for human communications and to pro-vide much of this faculty training.

Skills for Humanizing the Electronic Classroom

Moving beyond basic use of the technology, faculty should be able to approximate a more interactive, comfortable, learner-centered envi-ronment in the electronic classroom. In other words, different skills are needed for rapport-building at a distance. "Humanizing" means creating "an accepting classroom environment" that attempts to reduce the barri-ers of technology and geographic distance, and enhance instructor-learner and learner-learner rapport (Parker & Monson, 1980, p. 2). For many faculty, the need to humanize distance classrooms requires using new interactive, collaborative teaching approaches (or using these approaches more extensively).

Examples include (Jonassen & Hannum, 1987; Willis, 1992):

- Icebreaker exercises, student introductions, and in-class ex-plorations of learner expectations
- Asking students to describe previous distance learning expe-riences and suggestions for peers who are newer to distance learning courses
- Collecting student information using questionnaires and shar-ing a summary in class
- Collecting student photographs to be shown in-class or online
- Personalizing classroom exchanges by using student names

- Improving one's presentation skills before the camera in order to enhance the experience of instructor-learner eye contact and connection

Student affairs staff will be required to provide training programs and orientations for distance faculty, as well as individualized consultation to guide instructors who need to acquire new skills to make their classroom (and online) styles more interactive, engaging, or warm.

Revising Teaching to Emphasize Active Learning

Traditional lecture formats are less effective for engaging students, maintaining interest and motivation, addressing adult learner needs, and producing learning outcomes in the distance classroom. Reliance on the more traditional lecture format, in which students adopt a mostly passive role, tends to lead to distance learner under-involvement and disconnectedness from the course content and class experience (Banks & Banks, 1995). Instead, distance instructors will need to adopt new teaching methods that fall under the heading of "active learning" (Johnson, Johnson, & Smith, 1991, p. 1; Silberman, 1996, p. 1). Active learning strategies intentionally produce more learner participation and instructor-learner interactions and result in higher distance learner motivation (Bland, et al., 1992; Price, Repman, & White, 1994) and greater learning outcomes (Jonassen & Hannum, 1987; Keller, 1983). Examples of active learning approaches for academic classrooms include the following:

- *Classroom discussion*, in comparison with classroom lecture, is a basic method for stimulating learner interest and reflection on course content (Schomberg, 1988; Weimer, 1993). Classroom discussion (in televised courses or online) tends to meet the learning needs of adult learners. In the televised classroom, the instructor must take a strong role initiating, facilitating, and concluding discussions. Classroom discussion methods include interspersing lecture with discussion throughout a class meeting, addressing specific students or geographic groups, or asking students to write down on paper their responses to an issue before beginning the discussion.

- *Cooperative learning*, which is the instructional use of small groups. Learners in small classroom groups share goals and strive for mutual learning outcomes. Cooperative learning groups emphasize interdependent learning, so that student success is partly tied to the success of other group members (Johnson, Johnson, & Holubec, 1990). For instance, students in a math course may form a small group to solve a problem; sociology students may form a group to conduct a case analysis of a family; business students and nursing students may use group simulations to gain practice responding to real-life problems; and a philosophy class might use small groups to debate ethics and values conflicts.

- *Role plays*, especially in skills-based courses, can be used to demonstrate certain points, make course content more meaningful and relevant, and enliven the televised interactive classroom experience. Role plays provide in-class illustrations and allow for supervised practice. For instance, students in communications courses may role-play interactions found in business settings; student counselors may role-play counselor/client interactions in a counseling methods class; or MBA students may role-play administrative situations. Instructors can also use *demonstration or modeling* techniques by taking part in role-plays.

- *Directed questions* can be used in combination with short lectures, discussions, cooperative group activities, and role-plays to narrow, redirect, or highlight course material; to promote learner interest, attention, and interaction; and to guide deeper reflection on course content (Johnson, Johnson, & Smith, 1991; Silberman, 1996). For example, directed questions allow the distance instructor to ask about students to react to course material, solve a problem, or generate a hypothesis. Questions can be used to promote class cohesion in interactive televised classrooms. The instructor uses active efforts to promote learner-learner interactions by asking students to react to the responses of peers. Directed questions also are a basis for online course discussions and chat rooms.

Student affairs staff generally are experts using active learning methods outside the classroom in student development programs and when student services are provided in groups (e.g., career decision groups). An important new assignment will be to provide main campus faculty with professional development workshops in which they learn about and practice new teaching methods. Table 5.1 shows the outline of one institution's distance faculty in-service training program.

Table 5.1
Faculty Development for Distance Learning:
"Teaching On Television Workshop Series"

Monday
- Materials Distribution; Studio Facilities Tour; Logistics of TV Classes
- Who is the Distance Learner?[1]

Tuesday
- Classroom Interaction with Distance Students[1]
- Teaching Strategies to Promote Interaction[1]
- Designing Effective Visuals for Television; Library Resources; Copyright Issues

Wednesday
- Roles of Site Directors[1,2]
- Faculty/Site Director Meetings and Discussions[1,2]
- Panel of "Veteran" Distance Instructors

Thursday
- Practice Teaching in the Studio Classroom

1. Areas of student affairs professionals expertise
2. Site Directors who are distance student services generalists

Academic Liaison

[A potential pitfall of the expanding use of educational technology is that communication can become] impersonal, routinized, or standardized [and sometimes technology allows communications that are] really not appropriate to a particular [student] situation . . .

This is just the opposite of the "high touch" service most student affairs offices try to provide. (Strong, 1994, p. 12)

One traditional student affairs role has been to serve as a liaison between students and the campus—between learners and various student services, learners and institutional leaders, and on occasion, learners and faculty or academic departments. For example, advisors or residence staff may help new students to negotiate several campus offices in pursuit of registration, financial aid, and work-study opportunities; student affairs officers may represent the institution at judicial hearings and student concerns meetings; and counselors may serve as consultants for faculty when personal concerns interfere with a student's classroom performance. This role will be greatly expanded for professionals working in distance learning settings. Academic liaison responsibilities will include: a mediation function, assisting communications between students and individual instructors; an advising function, assisting students in their communications with academic departments; an administrative function, assisting student communications with the institution; and an learning-environment manager function, assisting with student negotiation of the overall academic program at a distance.

Communications Mediator

As communications mediators, student affairs professionals will be much more involved in academic interactions between faculty and distance students. Student affairs staff on the main campus (distance learning advisors, mentors, or directors) or at distance sites (site director generalists) will need to be available, for example, to help students understand course syllabi or class requirements, generate solutions to problems completing coursework, work through electronic classroom experiences, and prepare most effectively for tests or exams. Although faculty will continue to perform these tasks as well, they will not always have the office-time availability of student affairs staff, they will not be on-site as distance site directors are, and they are likely to have heavier teaching loads due to the capacity for larger enrollments via distance formats. Faculty will be available via email; however, students sometimes will be unable or unwilling to wait for the delayed responses of asynchronous communication.

Advisor-Liaison

As advisor-liaisons, student affairs staff will be much more involved in the student's relationship with his or her academic department or educational program. Student affairs generalists will need to advise students about course scheduling, registration tasks, etc. They also will need to supervise student's progression through degree programs—ensuring that learners follow academic prerequisites, co-requisites, and basic competency requirements for various courses, as determined by a program's departmental faculty. Although student affairs professionals work as academic advisors on traditional campuses, they will be a primary contact with more responsibility for following the student's academic progression in the distance setting. Similarly, they will tend to be more involved in making decisions regarding transfer credits, course waivers, credits for life experience, etc.

Administrator-Representative

As administrators, student affairs professionals will be institutional leaders and institutional representatives in geographically distant locations. In some program arrangements, they will appear to be one-person student affairs operations—providing services from marketing and admissions to records and registration, to academic advising and support, to career planning and placement, to graduation certification and exit. They will tend to have more decision-making responsibility. Further, when students concerns arise—e.g., course grade appeals, requests for exemptions from class attendance, moving between main-campus and distance-learning courses and programs, financial aid waivers—distance student affairs staff will assist the student in his or her interactions with (distance site, main campus, or online) institutional offices. Although residence hall directors, mentors, first-year advisors, and other staff serve in this sort of administrative ombudsperson role on traditional campuses, the distance student affairs staff will be making more determinations and doing more to help learners connect with the main campus and interpret information.

Learning Environment Manager

Finally, all of these academic liaison functions combine so that distance student affairs staff serve as key players in helping create a good overall fit between the individual learner and the institution, distance program, academic degree, and course progression he or she undertakes. Distance student services staff will have responsibility for managing the institution's distance learning environment—including electronically delivered courses and services as well as those located at distance sites; including student services as well as electronic classroom experiences; and including learners' interactions with distance staff, faculty, and peer learners. Institutional leaders will expect distance services staff to ensure that the learning environment attracts, keeps, and produces positive learning outcomes among its distance learner constituency. It will be their job to build the "new relationships with learners" required for successful programs.

Program Designer

"Learners will select a variety of instructional formats depending on a number of factors including . . . degree of fit between the requirements of the delivery and the life circumstances of the learner" (Duning, Van Kekerix, & Zaborowski, 1993, p. 251). The design of distance learning programs typically occurs at two levels: (a) institutions apply innovations to the overall delivery of their higher education offerings in order to create an entire institution-wide distance learning program, and (b) academic departments apply innovations to their curricula, and sometimes alter or reformulate courses and curricula, in order to create degree programs or course offerings that will fit into their institution's distance learning format (Duning, Van Kekerix, & Zaborowski, 1993; Keast, 1997; Smith & Kelly, 1987). Correspondingly, student affairs professionals, particularly senior student affairs administrators, are (a) likely to become increasingly involved with the design of institution-wide distance learning units, and (b) likely to work more closely with academic programs as they design (or redesign) their curricula and courses to be delivered via distance learning.

Designing Distance Learning Units

At most institutions, implementing distance learning programs means bringing about change in how the institution views its academic offerings, teaching/learning functions, and student populations. Designing, implementing, and maintaining distance learning at an institution usually takes place in four stages (Duning, et al., 1993):

1. An *entrepreneurial stage* which involves bringing the new distance program into existence, including finding/allocating resources, building the technological infrastructure (online systems, websites, interactive classrooms, etc.), training staff and faculty, securing institutional commitment, enrolling distance students, and other start-up tasks.
2. A *collectivity stage* which involves implementing the program more securely, and putting the resources in place to be able to "produce the new educational product on an ongoing and sustained basis" (Duning, et al., 1993, p. 105).
3. A *formalization stage* which involves creating a larger, usu ally more complex and hierarchical, organizational structure to manage the program as it becomes larger, has greater enrollments, and delivers academic offerings through a greater variety of technologies.
4. A *latter stage* that can result in program renewal and growth, stabilization and maintenance, or decline over time.

The entrepreneurial and collectivity stages are a period of planning, designing, and experimenting. These stages require (Jones & Lewis, 1991; Keast, 1997):

*   Comprehensive planning that takes into account multiple factors and variables, and bases decisions on research knowledge, information about existing program successes, and evaluation findings.

- Collective change in approaches, beliefs and attitudes, and cooperation throughout the institution—from top administrators to individual faculty and staff.
- An "interventionist" mindset (Keast, 1997, p. 44), by which institutional members set out to strategically and systematically follow a logical plan of action to reach a clear, specific objective.

At this point in the life of a new distance learning program, both technology experts and student development/student services experts will be needed to make plans for, and implement, the institution's vision for a new unit that will attract, enroll, retain, and produce successes and outcomes among a new student population. Student affairs professionals, in particular, will be needed to determine methods for marketing to and retaining distance learners, and for offering the services or support needed to promote learner success.

The formalization stage is a period of institutionalizing and setting up a system for tighter controls over a growing distance learning organization within the institution. It comes about in response to growth in the distance learning program's size and complexity, and in response to growing pressures that are a result of increasing demands from students or other outside constituencies (Duning, et al., 1993). Formalization results in a more complex organizational structure: larger teaching, student support, and administrative staffs; more managers to whom the larger staffs reports; less familiarity and less contact between the front-line staff and upper management; and the addition of more specialists— in narrower, more specialized areas of technology, audio-video production, and student services (Keast, 1997). Student affairs professionals will be needed at this stage (a) to fill the majority of mid-management roles, (b) to work as distance student services specialists, and (c) to be liaisons between technicians/technology staff, and instructors and other human resource staff.

In the latter stages, programs thrive or decline. In order to thrive, leaders and managers must (Keast, 1997, p. 42):

- be flexible; respond to feedback from faculty, staff, students, and other constituencies; and learn from experience how to revise distance offerings so that the distance program's organizational structure will function as effectively as possible.

- collaborate with key stakeholders (learners, faculty) and decision-makers (top administration, institutional leaders, funding sources), so that everyone involved in the operation understands and assimilates how the distance operation functions, how its goals and needs change over time, and how to best respond in order to keep it thriving.

Two key elements required in the latter stages for a successful, maturing distance learning program are technology experts and high-quality distance faculty. The third required element is strong organizational management. Here, seasoned student affairs professionals, particularly mid-level and upper-level directors who have experience in formal or informal internal consultant roles on the traditional campus, will be needed to fill critical positions providing ongoing leadership for more mature distance learning units.

Designing or Redesigning Academic Programs

Academic departments and their teaching faculty have responsibility for transforming main-campus instructional offerings into courses and degree-programs that fit into the instructional technology of distance learning. This process involves addressing certain challenges, such as: maintaining academic standards (Kirby & Garrison, 1989); identifying methods for adequate instructor/learner interactions, delivering high-quality instructional programs, and designing effective course materials (Johnson & Silvernail, 1990; McNeil, 1990); revising faculty roles in the learning process (Dillon & Walsh, 1992); and addressing nuts-and-bolts concerns such as delivering instructional materials, back-and-forth delivery of student work, and copyrights of written materials, broadcasts, and online intellectual products (Cyrs, 1997).

Traditionally, the design of academic degree programs and departmental curricula has been focused on traditional college student populations and their learning needs and goals. Academic faculty at four-year institutions generally have less experience designing programs to meet the needs, goals, and life situations of a wider, more diverse, less traditional learner population. As a result, student affairs professionals who are experts in the area of learning needs and responding to diverse learner populations, or who have experience with community college models that can contribute to distance program design at four-year institutions, increasingly will be asked to collaborate with academic departments as they adapt curricula to be more amenable to "student-centered learning activities", "new instructional technology", and fundamental changes in how professors "contribute to the teaching-learning process" (Beaudoin, 1990, p. 2; Schwitzer, 1998, November).

For example, we believe departmental faculty and student affairs will collaborate more in the distance learning arena than they typically do on traditional campuses, as they deal with the following issues, questions, and decisions (Ancis, 1997; Brown, 1996; Perry, 1977; Schwitzer, 1998, November; Tunstall, 1973):

1. *Admissions, Setting Standards, Continuance, Program Completion*—Institutions typically set admissions standards to the college or university, while academic departments set admission, continuance, and completion requirements for specific degree programs. Departments moving into distance learning must formalize and disseminate program admission and completion requirements before the program is "on air" or "online". Decisions include whether (or how) to modify requirements to attract and build a distance learner consumer base; whether standards should build in more flexibility or variability in order to respond to varying learner situations; how to change time-line expectations for reaching program milestones; how standards for continuance, academic probation, suspension, and reinstatement should be written to apply fairly to learners in different types of electronically delivered programs; and how to evaluate the progress of students who complete courses occasionally and irregularly around other life demands. Collaboration between academic departments and student development practitioners will be needed in many circumstances to develop an approach that will maintain academic rigor while at the same time addressing learner characteristics and needs.

2. *Transfer Credits, Testing Out, Credit for Life Experiences*—Academic programs typically have provisions for the occasional student who receives credit for, or has waived, a course or competency (e.g., general math requirements) through testing out, AP credits brought from high school, or transfer credits from community college or a four-year institution. However, distance learners typically bring more prior college-level academic experience, professional competencies, and life experiences to their academic pursuits. As a result, distance learners are more likely to seek credit or waiver for degree requirements as a result of

transfer credits, placing out, and life experience. Departments must set policies and procedures for each of these, which will occur with more regularity than experienced with more traditional learners. Student affairs professionals, working with academic departments, will be needed to advise students, educate them about options, develop portfolios of life experience, and assist with constructing more individualized overall learning plans.

3. *Prerequisites, Course Sequencing, Course Substitutions, Course Waivers, Class Attendance*—Academic degree programs typically are constructed to follow a pre-set, organized, relatively unchanging sequence of courses. Courses usually progress from more basic and general to more advanced and specific. In turn, earlier courses serve as prerequisites for later courses, and co-requisite courses may need to be taken together in the same semester. Although special allowances may be granted in students' course sequences, it is expected that they will primarily follow the established academic program. However, distance learners may tend to need more flexibility in course sequencing (a) when constrictions such as interactive televised air-time or online site availability limit the number and variety of courses a department offers each semester or limit the scheduling of specific courses, and (b) when competing life circumstances interfere with the learner's ability to pursue the normal course progression. Similarly, distance learners with prior academic experience (e.g., an associate degree or earlier coursework in a similar field of study) and advanced life or work experience tend to request more individualized opportunities to waive certain prerequisites or to make substitutions in course requirements—even when they do not formally test out of courses or receive transfer or life experience credits.

A related issue is whether, or when, students may be permitted to complete certain courses by viewing videotapes of class meetings or online records of web-based class meetings—rather than actually attending and participating in the electronic classroom experience. In some cases, distance learning offerings are *intended* to be completed independently and according to the individual learner's schedule and pace. However, when an electronic format is used to recreate the classroom experience, and therefore attendance and participation are expected and required, faculty will be faced with the question of extenuating circumstances, evaluating absences, making allowances, etc.

Yet another related issue is how to set and maintain advising, registration, and other institutional or departmental deadlines from a distance, while at the same responding to some learners' needs for more flexible deadlines or nontraditional academic calendars.

In all of these areas, academic departments increasingly will collaborate or consult with student development experts in the institution's distance learning administration or distance student services unit when decisions are made about how to maintain a program's basic structure and integrity, while responding as realistically as possible to the more individualized needs and experiences of adult distance learners.

4. Changes in Academic Requirements—The transition to distance formats may require some change in exact academic requirements, such as: less reliance on formal writing, but more reliance on informal writing-to-learn activities, particularly in online exchanges; less reliance on formal tests and other traditional methods of student evaluation, but more reliance on developing final projects and products; less reliance on face-to-face exchanges, but more reliance on videotaped presentations and other asynchronous demonstrations of learning outcomes. Some changes will be required because distance learning courses will be much larger than main-campus classes, resulting in larger instructor workloads. Other changes will be needed as adjustments are made to the reduced opportunity for face-to-face instructor-learner contact (Keast, 1997). As we discussed earlier, student affairs professionals will provide one source of expert advice as departmental faculty examine new methods of setting and measuring student learning outcomes.

A corresponding issue is how to provide supervision of distance learners in practica, internships, service-learning settings, or other field placements that are an integral, required part of a degree program, such as student nursing or student teaching—or how to change the requirement for field experiences to fit into the distance format. As we discussed earlier, when they are qualified, distance student services generalists who are assigned to geographically distance academic centers may provide field supervision of learners in some academic majors or degrees— as part of their normal duties, as adjunct instructors, or through another arrangement.

Outcome Evaluator

"Distance education can be an expensive proposition, so it needs new methods for demonstrating its effectiveness" (Cyrs, 1997, p. ii). In

general, the research literature supports the notion that distance education can be an effective format for teaching and learning (Hanson &
Maushak, 1996). However, multiple institutional constituencies—including top administration, academic departments and their individual distance faculty, distance-student consumers, as well as boards of visitors,
legislators, and other governing or funding bodies—have a need to know
(or are invested in) whether a *particular* distance learning program at *a
particular* institution is operating as planned, is operating efficiently,
and is producing intended learning outcomes (Kozloff, 1987; Schwitzer,
1997). In turn, another role for student affairs professionals working as
distance site directors, distance student services providers, distance learning unit managers and leaders, or assessment specialists will be evaluation of the distance learning enterprises with which they are involved.

Different types of evaluation will be required depending on where
the institution's distance learning program is in its development. In sum,
evaluation will be needed to determine the following: (a) implementation success, (b) intermediate-level learning outcomes, and (c) ultimate-
level student outcomes (Patton, 1986; Suchman, 1967).

First, *implementation-level outcome goals* are related to successful
implementation of specific components of the program or overall distance learning project (Patton, 1986), such as getting specific degree
programs underway or a particular delivery technology up-and-running.
Measures of implementation sometimes are referred to as producing "formative data" (Simonson, 1997, p. 88). This level of evaluation answers
the basic questions: Was the program put into place as planned? Did
learners enroll and utilize the academic programs as planned? How satisfied were the learners? Measures of activity (e.g., How many courses
were produced?, How many students were served?) and efficiency (e.g.,
How many students were successful?, How many students enrolled in
additional courses?, How much did the course delivery cost and how
much tuition was generated?) are a part of implementation-level evaluation (Woodley & Kirkwood, 1986). Methodologically, descriptive measures, satisfaction surveys, and student evaluations generally are used
(Schwitzer, 1997; 1998). Evaluating implementation is most important
for new distance learning projects or for programs undergoing significant change in delivery format or course offerings; however, implementation-level evaluation also tends to be part of ongoing assessment. Implementation questions are important to all constituencies (university leaders,

program managers, distance faculty, learners), since successful program implementation is a prerequisite for producing subsequent results, such as learning and other student outcomes. Learners and potential students are particularly interested in whether a program is smoothly operating and able to effectively meet their needs and objectives.

Second, *intermediate-level outcome goals* are related to learning in specific courses and at specific steps along the way in a degree program. These learning goals include increased topical knowledge, increased understanding, new skills, and application of specific course material (Patton, 1986; Schwitzer, 1997; 1998). In other words, evaluating intermediate outcomes answers the question: Did the learning experience make a difference? (Simonson, 1997). This type of evaluation information is sometimes referred to as "summative data" (Simonson, 1997, p. 88). Methodologically, post-course measures of knowledge of course content or, where possible, pre-post comparisons of new learning from course experiences are generally used (Schwitzer, 1998). Course grades, test scores, and other student performance measures also are used. Intermediate measures of learning outcomes are most important when evaluating new course offerings, courses that are attracting a changing student population, or courses offered via changing delivery systems; however, intermediate learning outcome data also is part of ongoing evaluation. Intermediate learning outcomes are important to all constituencies; however, typically they are most important and of the most interest to academic departments and distance faculty, who are invested in determined whether new delivery formats are providing successful learning experiences, or learning experiences comparable to main campus courses.

Third, *ultimate-level goals* follow next in the operational chain of intended outcomes (Patton, 1986; Suchman, 1967). Ultimate goals are related to broader or longer-term objectives—usually (a) academic success over time, retention, and graduation or program completion, which should result in (b) accomplishing student outcomes such as positive changes in work situations (salary increases, promotions, desirable career changes) or personal situations (achieving personal development goals) (Kozloff, 1987). In other words, ultimate-level evaluation answers the question: Were there positive consequences for a student who enrolled in, persevered, and completed a successfully implemented distance learning program? Methodologically, measures used for this outcome level are institutional data such as retention and completion rates, and student reports of life-change and goal- accomplishment. Although all constituencies have interest in ultimate outcomes, they tend to be the data of most interest and importance to institutional leaders, administrators, governing bodies and funding sources (Schwitzer, 1998).

Key elements of distance learning assessment are: evaluating program implementation, demonstrating learning outcomes, and showing that a distance learning enterprise is producing desired outcomes in students' lives outside the academic setting. This type of measurement and evaluation will be conducted by student affairs professionals who have the skills and experience to:

- translate distance learning program goals into measurable outcomes,
- provide the kind of information multiple institutional constituencies usually seek from assessment, and
- produce evaluation data that can be communicated successfully to various audiences in written reports and oral presentations.

Case Illustration: Student Support in One Institution's Distance Program

"Different institutions may develop different answers to . . . assess existing learner-centered distance designs, build upon those designs, create new practices, and implement these practices with the learning needs of [their students] in mind" (LeBaron & Bragg, 1994). The main focus of the distance learning research and professional literature published so far has been on telecommunications and information technology—the hard-wired component of distance learning. Less has been written about student development and learner support in the distance context. By comparison, our focus is on the growing recognition that, in general, learners also require supportive services in order to make the distance college adjustment, and to learn and experience development at a distance. This final section draws on earlier discussions in this book to illustrate the implementation of one conceptual model of distance student services at one institution.

Program Design

The distance learning program at Old Dominion, called Teletechnet, relies mainly on satellite-delivered, two-way audio and one-way or two-way video interactive classrooms to deliver as a true a *facsimile* as possible of the main campus college classroom experience. Courses in more than a dozen bachelor's and master's degree programs are broadcast from a studio classroom on the main campus in Norfolk, VA (with a live main campus class in attendance) to special receptor classrooms located on dozens of community college sites across the state, to receptor classrooms at community college campuses in neighboring and partner states, and to business and military sites. In Virginia, students, mostly nontraditional learners, complete their first two college years and all of their general education requirements at their local community college. An articulation agreement allows them to then transfer their Associates Degree credits to ODU, select a major, and complete all their remaining courses via Teletechnet right in their community. A typical course has up to twenty students in the main campus classroom, one to ten or more students at each distance site, and a total class size averaging 90 students, but it is not unusual to find classes as large as 160.

Distance Site Directors: Student Services Generalist

The Teletechnet program was designed to provide a reasonable *facsimile* of main campus student services and institutional support. The basic arrangement is that each distance site has a full-time college student affairs generalist and an assistant, who administer the program locally, conduct admissions and orientation, advise and mentor local learners, and provide general oversight of academic program reception at their location.

Site Directors are master's-level professionals with degrees in college student affairs administration, college counseling, or business administration. Site Directors act as administrators, student affairs officers, advisors, counselors, resource managers (for bookstore materials, textbooks, coursepaks), student conduct and honor system leaders, and more. They recruit and hold informational college nights. Sometimes they act as guidance counselors and academic skills tutors.

Site Directors also hire and supervise proctors who are present while students take exams; coordinate videotape lending and duplicating for students who miss a class meeting or want a copy to review; and direct exam make-up dates held periodically.

In terms of physical plant, Site Directors maintain Old Dominion University offices provided on the community college campus, and oversee ODU Teletechnet receptor classrooms provided in community college buildings. For professional support, they attend a weekly two-way interactive distance student affairs video-conference delivered by main campus program administrators, and travel to campus for periodic meetings.

Professional Development and Support of Faculty

The academic programs delivered through Teletechnet are the very same as those offered on the main campus; the same prerequisites, course requirements, course content, and exit requirements apply. Regular full-time and adjunct faculty who teach on the main campus are recruited for Teletechnet. At ODU, there is an effort to recognize distance teaching. Faculty are encouraged to distance teach, are allowed course releases to prepare for new distance learning courses, and when classes are very large, they are eligible for a stipend and graduate teaching assistance. Distance teaching is a valued and important part of the tenure and promotion review.

Further, first-timers attend an extensive training program led by instructional television personnel, student affairs staff, and other faculty. Ongoing professional workshops occur to provide more advanced training. Other institutional support is provided to help with computer-driven visual presentations, creating Websites, and using other media.

Admissions, Registrar, and Orientation

Distance learners must meet the same admissions criteria as other students at the university. The community-college articulation agreements allows those with the Associates Degree to receive general studies credit for distance learning or enrollment on the main campus. While admissions is handled centrally on the main campus, the Site Directors do most of the leg work of recruitment and admissions counseling. They also provide orientation for new students in one-on-one interviews, cohort group meetings, and/or by videotape.

Once enrolled, distance learners receive course schedules and registration materials each semester by mail. They also have materials available for pick-up at their local sites, and can access the same material online from their home. Teletechnet programs publish three-year academic schedule plans, so that the nontraditional learner can make long-range plans around their work and family responsibilities.

Advising, Career Counseling, and Program Planning

Advising and Program Planning come from two sources: Site Directors conduct a lot of the work in person, helping students understand course sequences and developing their long-range plans for completing their degrees. In addition, every distance learning program has one or more academic advisors housed on the main campus who is dedicated to Teletechnet advising. Toll-free phone lines, email accounts, fax, and established office hours provide each distance learner with access to his or her own academic advisor. Each semester, they can review their degree requirements and plan course schedules as would main campus academic advisees.

The main campus Career Management Office provides nearly all of its services online with easy access for distance learners, including job and interview preparation, placement listings and employer listings, internship and field placements, and career planning. Career Management staff are assigned to work closely with the Teletechnet program via telephone, email, Websites, and periodic visits.

Library, Bookstore, Course Materials, and Textbook Services

Each distance learning course provides learners with all needed course materials—syllabus, reading lists, assignments, handouts for the semester, journal articles, class activities—either through a prepared package that students purchase when the semester begins, or through an online Website. The main campus bookstore orders and delivers textbooks to distance sites. And nearly all library services are available online. There is one central office on the main campus dedicated to handling distance learner textbooks and prepackaged course notes.

Interaction with Faculty, Staff, and Peers

The Teletechnet program emphasizes interactivity. (The institution also is adding an electronic course program, which, while it will provide another consumer option and increase flexibility for some learners, will not provide the kind of college experience facsimile the Teletechnet program offers.) Distance learners have access to faculty: (1) in the interactive classroom, where they can see, hear, and talk to the instructor; (2) during class breaks, when dedicated phone-lines to the instructor are available; (3) using dedicated toll-free phones and voice-mail provided for each instructor, with an emphasis on interactions during established telephone office hours; and (4) by email.

For interactions with staff, learners have access to (1) site directors during flexible office hours; (2) all main-campus personnel during regular university business hours, by telephone and fax; (3) their main-campus academic advisors; and (4) administrators and staff in all of the Teletechnet program offices on the main campus (textbook office, mailing and delivery station, instructional television) at any time via email or during regular business hours by telephone and fax.

Learners interact with each other in class using two-way communications (microphones and sometimes video monitors); with others at their locality in-class, outside of class, by telephone for group projects, in support groups held on-site, and in student-led groups that emerge off-site.

Distribution of Materials

Because timely and efficient distribution of materials is of special concern to distance learners and affects their experience, it deserves separate mention. The coursepaks coordinated by the main campus office are printed and delivered by mail to the distance sites or directly to students' homes by a commercial vendor, and bookstore-ordered texts are similarly delivered to distance sites by the publisher.

A separate office handles only distribution of written materials between the main campus and sites. This is a full-time job for several staff! Exams, attendance records, student papers and assignments at one end, and graded assignments and tests, personal communications, and instructor feedback at the other end, are delivered back-and-forth between sites and the main campus daily using Federal Express. The central main-campus office then distributes incoming mail to individual instructors across campus using the daily campus mail system or hand-delivery.

Community College Resources: Counseling and Student Affairs

The Teletechnet program is somewhat unique because most of the special, dedicated electronic receptor classrooms to which the courses are delivered are housed on community college campuses, and most distance learners in the program were previously enrolled at the community college where they now attend distance classes. As a result, in many cases, the distance student are allowed access to the community college's counseling and student affairs services. This unusual arrangement is unlikely in most distance programs, because it requires a close formal relationship between the main institution and local community colleges. Further, when programs such as ODU's Teletechnet are delivered into students' homes or individual work-places through broadcast or cable television or Internet—rather than to centralized group settings such as receptor classrooms—it is less likely that learners will have access to local counseling and student affairs supports. In this case, online and telephone support services delivered from the main campus are more likely. When this trend is followed, institutions and their distance learners trade the benefits of greater flexibility in scheduling and fewer travel constraints that come with individualized home delivery of higher education, on one hand, with the drawback of having available fewer in-person student support services when they are needed.

Including Distance Learners in University Life

The Teletechnet program attempts to establish as many connections as possible between the distance learner and institution. In some communities where distance courses are delivered, there are local study groups, tutoring or mentoring meetings (such as for engineering students), supportive seminars for students in internships and field placements (such as in nursing and special education), and professional/academic major club activities. There are student activities in distance communities, mostly centering around learners' academic and career interests: career gatherings, professional development lectures and work-shops, and academic support groups and services. These may organized and facilitated by Site Directors, local and visiting adjunct instructors (such as field placement supervisors), the university's continuing education program, or students themselves. The university also uses two ideas described above to bring a campus community to distance sites: (1) combining main-campus recruiting trips that take institutional leaders, student affairs staff, and faculty across the state with "college night" type visits to distance learning sites, and (2) televised graduation ceremonies held each May for distance graduates. Further, main-campus distance program leaders, including vice presidents, academic deans, faculty, and student affairs staff, make regular field trips to visit site directors and students at distance sites.

All in all, the Teletechnet program combines telecommunications technology in the electronic classroom, computer technology, in-person site administration and guidance, access to main campus student services, access to instructors, and field visiting to provide needed distance support services and include the university's distance participants in its institutional life.

References

American College Personnel Association (1994). *Student learning imperative: Implications for student affairs*. Washington, DC: Author.

Ancis, J. R. (1997). *Teletechnet assessment report: Human services counseling program*. Norfolk, VA: Old Dominion University, Department of Educational Leadership and Counseling.

Astin, A. W. (1985). *Achieving educational excellence*. San Francisco: Jossey-Bass.

Astin, A. W. (1993). *What matters in college: Four critical years revisited*. San Francisco: Jossey-Bass.

Banks, C. A. M., & Banks, J. A. (1995). Equity pedagogy: An essential component of multicultural education. *Theory Into Practice, 34,* (3), 152-158.

Beaudoin, M. F. (1990). The instructor's changing role in distance education. *The American Journal of Distance Education, 4,* (2) 21-29.

Bland, K. P., Morrison, G. R., & Ross, S. M. (1992, November). *Student attitudes toward learning link: A distance education project.* Paper presented at the meeting of the Mid-South Educational Research Association. Knoxville, TN.

Brown, N. (1996, August). Administering distance learning programs. In J. R. Ancis, *Interactive-television and multimedia classrooms: Teaching psychology at a distance.* Symposium presented at the annual meeting of the American Psychological Association, Toronto, Ontario, Canada.

Burge, E., and Howard, J. L. (1990). Audio-conferencing in graduate education: A case study. *American Journal of Distance Education, 4,* (2) 3 - 13.

Creamer, D.(Ed.). (1990). *College student development: Theory and practice for the 1990s.* Washington, DC: American College Personnel Association.

Cyrs, T. E. (Ed.). (1997). *Teaching and learning at a distance: What it takes to effectively design, deliver, and evaluate programs.* San Francisco: Jossey-Bass.

Dillon, C. L., and Walsh, S. M. (1992). Faculty: The neglected resource in distance education. *The American Journal of Distance Education, 6,* (3) 5-21.

Duning, B. S., Van Kekerix, M. J., and Zaborowski, L. M. (1993). *Reaching learners through telecommunications.*

Fried, J. (Ed.). (1995). *Shifting paradigms in student affairs: Culture, context, teaching, and learning.* Washington, DC: American College Personnel Association.

Hanson, D., & Maushak, N. (1996). *Distance education: Review of the literature.* Ames, Iowa: Research Institute for Studies in Education.

Johnson, D. W., Johnson, R., & Holubec, E. (1990). *Circles of learning: Cooperation in the classroom.* Edina, MN: Interaction Book Company.

Johnson, D. W., Johnson, R. T., & Smith, K. A. (1991). *Active learning: Cooperation in the classroom.* Edina, MN: Interaction Book Company.

Johnson, J. L., & Silvernail, D. L. (1990). *Report of faculty perceptions of Community College of Maine Instructional Television Systems, Fall 1989.* University of Southern Maine.

Jonassen, D. H., & Hannum, W. C. (1987, December). Research-based principles for designing computer software. *Instructional Technology,* 7-14.

Jones, P., & Lewis, J. (1991). Implementing a strategy for collective change in higher education. *Studies in Higher Education, 16,* (1) 51-61.

Keast, D. A. (1997). Toward an effective model for implementing distance education programs. *The American Journal of Distance Education, 11,* (2) 39-55.

Keller, J. M. (1983). Motivational design of instruction. In C. M. Reigeluth (Ed.), *Instructional-design theories and models* (pp. 383-436). Hillsdale, NJ: Erlbaum.

Kirby, D. M., & Garrison, D. R. (1989). Graduate distance education: A study of the aims and delivery systems. In *Proceedings of the Eighth Annual Conference of the Canadian Association for the Study of Adult Education.* Cornwall, Ontario: Saint Lawrence College of Saint Laurent.

Knefelkamp, L., Widick, C., & Parker, C. A. (Eds.). (1978). *Applying new developmental findings.* San Francisco: Jossey-Bass.

Kozloff, J. (1987). A student-centered approach to accountability and assessment. *Journal of College Student Personnel, 28,* 419-424.

LeBaron, J. E., & Bragg, C. A. (1994). Practicing what we preach: Creating distance education models to prepare teachers for the twenty-first century. *The American Journal of Distance Education, 8,* (1), 5-19.

McNeil, D. R. (1990). *Wiring the ivory tower: A round table on technology in higher education.* Washington, DC: Academy for Educational Development.

Overbaugh, R. C. (1994). Research-based guidelines for computer-based instruction development. *Journal of Research on Computing in Education, 27,* (1) 29-47.

Parker, L., & Monson, M. (1980). *Teletechniques: An instructional model for interactive conferencing.* The Directional Design Library, 38. New Jersey: Educational Technology Publications.

Pascarelli, E. T., & Terenzini, P. T. (1991). *How college effects students.* San Francisco: Jossey-Bass.

Patton, M. Q. (1986). *Utilization-focused evaluation* (2nd ed.). Beverly Hills, CA: Sage.

Perry, W. (1977). *The open university: History and evaluation of a dynamic innovation in higher education.* San Francisco: Jossey-Bass.

Price, R. V., Repman, J., and White, D. (1994). Producing effective graduate-level distance education courses for interactive television.

Proceedings of Selected Research and Development Presentations at the 1994 National Convention of the Association for Educational Communications and Technology, Nashville, TN, 641-664.

Schwitzer, A. M. (1997). Utilization-focused evaluation: Proposing a useful method of program evaluation for college counselors and student development professionals. *Measurement and Evaluation in Counseling and Development, 30,* 50 - 61.

Schwitzer, A. M. (1998). Applying the *Student Learning Imperative* to counseling center outcome evaluation. *Journal of College Student Psychotherapy, 13,* 71-92.

Schwitzer, A. M. (1998, November). Teaching at a distance. Paper presented at the annual conference on teaching and technology of the Southeastern Psychological Association, Harrisonburg, VA.

Schomberg, S. F. (1988). *Strategies for active teaching and learning in university classrooms.* Minneapolis: University of Minnesota.

Silberman, M. (1996). *Active learning: 101 strategies to teach any subject.* Boston: Allyn & Bacon.

Simonson, M. R. (1997). Evaluating teaching and learning at a distance. In T. E. Cyrs (Ed.). *Teaching and learning at a distance: What it takes to effectively design, deliver, and evaluate programs.* San Francisco: Jossey-Bass.

Smith, P., & Kelly, M. (Eds.). (1987). *Distance education and the mainstream.* New York: Croom Helm.

Stewart, D. (1987). Staff development needs in distance education and campused-based education: Are they so different? In P. Smith & M. Kelly (Eds.). *Distance education and the mainstream* pp. 156-174.

Strong, T. S. (1994). The technology and information explosion. In J. L. Baier & T. S. Strong (Eds.). *Technology in student affairs: Issues, applications, and trends.* Washington, DC: American College Personnel Association.

Suchman, E. A. (1967). *Evaluative research: Principles and practice in public service and social action programs.* New York: Russell Sage.

Tunstall, J. (Ed.). (1973). *The open university opens.* Amherst, MA: University of Amherst Press.

Weimer, M. (1993). *Improving your classroom teaching.* Newbury Park, CA: Sage.

Willis, B. (1992). Making distance learning effective: Key roles and responsibilities. *Educational Technology, 32,* 35-37.

Wolcott, L. L. (1995). The distance teacher as reflective practitioner. *Educational Technology*, January-February, 39 - 43.

Woodley, A., & Kirkwood, A. (1986). *Evaluation in distance learning*. Paper 10. Bletchley, England: Institute of Educational Technology, Open University (ED 304-122).

Afterward

We have attempted in this book to provide college student development professionals with information they need to promote learning and development among distance learners. Increasingly, the focus and priority of American education are on technology (Trotter, 1999) and the number of institutions with distance learning programs is growing rapidly (Moore, 1996). The reality of alternative educational systems that are wired via Internet, telecommunications technology, and other media and utilize new methods of teaching and learning has taken hold (Cummins & Sayers, 1995; Dede, 1996; LeBaron & Bragg, 1994).

Setting up and maintaining an institution's distance learning program is complex. It requires support from top administration, adequate resources for thorough planning and design, and careful selection of the appropriate technology and media to meet program goals and constituent learner needs (Moore, 1996; Keast, 1997). Part of the technology/media selection process is to "identify those educational functions that can be delivered better by technology than by people and thus release people to do those things that people do better than technology" (Moore, 1996; p. 4). What people do better than technology is create a "humane" interpersonal environment that supports distance learners (p. 4). In fact, although the primary focus often is on the technology, providing distance learner support "is as important as good [technical] design. . . . There is a direct relationship between the instructional effectiveness of a program and the time and money spent on learner support" (p. 4). Student affairs professionals must be prepared to provide needed distance learner support.

Distance learning requires active, engaging, meaningful teaching methods that enhance instruction in electronic classrooms in order to most effectively help students learn (Bland, Morrison, & Ross, 1992; Price, Repman, & White, 1994). Distance learning also is beginning to use new forms of communications, messages, and interpersonal interactions made possible by new multimedia formats (Dede & Lewis, 1995). For example, one emerging distance learning paradigm, "distributed education", complements face-to-face classroom interactions by using multimedia to engage students in computer-supported collaborative learning—such as having students work together by computer (ie., in virtual environments) to share information and solve simulated work- and life-problems (Dede, 1996; p. 4). In this way, new media and technologies allow students to have shared experiences of "learning-by-doing" (Dede, 1996; p. 6). Student development professionals also must be prepared to have more involvement with faculty and to play a larger role in academic life as institutions become more learner-centered when they deliver distance learning programs.

In the program illustration presented in Chapter 5, student affairs professionals used an innovative combination of roles and methods to provide learner and faculty support: Some staff were distance site directors, acting as student services generalists by operating local academic centers in communities away from the main campus. These distance student affairs generalists had responsibilities for admissions; academic advising, career counseling, and assistance with college adjustment; and registrar, record-keeping, and graduation tasks. By comparison, some staff were located at the institution's main campus, and provided academic advising and support across geographic distances via email and Internet, telephone and fax, mail, and audio-video conferencing. Selected main-campus personnel made occasional field visits to meet with students at distance sites. Still others provided consultation, training, support, and professional development for distance faculty and distance academic degree programs. "Setting in place a well-trained learner support network is essential for a successful distance education system" (Moore, 1996; p. 4)—in turn, student affairs professionals must retool themselves with the information, attitudes, and new skills required to design, set up, administer, and provide the varied distance student services and support functions their institutions will need.

References

Bland, K. P., Morrison, G. R., & Ross, S. M. (1992, November). *Student attitudes toward learning link: A distance education project.* Paper presented at the meeting of the Mid-South Educational Research Association. Knoxville, TN.

Cummins, J., & Sayers, D. (1995). *Brave new schools: Challenging cultural illiteracy through global learning machines.* New York: St. Martin's Press.

Dede, C. (1996). The evolution of distance education: Emerging technologies and distributed education. *The American Journal of Distance Education, 10,* 5–36.

Dede, C., & Lewis, M. (1995). *Assessment of emerging educational technologies that might assist and enhance school-to-work transitions.* Washington, DC: National Technical Information Services.

Keast, D. A. (1997). Toward an effective model for implementing distance education programs. *The American Journal of Distance Education, 11,* 39–55.

LeBaron, J. F., & Bragg, C. A. (1994). Practicing what we preach: Creating distance education models to prepare teachers for the twenty-first century. *The American Journal of Distance Education, 8,* 5–19.

Moore, M. G. (1996). Editorial: Tips for the manager setting up a distance education program. *The American Journal of Distance Education, 10,* 1 5.

Price, R. V., Repman, J., & White, D. (1994). Producing effective graduate-level distance education courses for interactive television. *Proceedings of Selected Research and Development Presentations at the 1994 National Convention of the Association for Educational Communications and Technology,* Nashville, TN, 641–664.

Trotter, A. (February 17, 1999). Congress expected to put high priority on technology. *Education Week.* 34–38.